W9-BZM-951

Butler Area Public Library

In Memory of
Charles E. McMichael, Sr.

Donor
The Egolfs

© DEMCO, INC.— Archive Safe

Butler Area Public Library
218 North McKean Street
Butler PA 16001

Just One Restless Rider

2794746

Butler Area Public Library
213 North McKean Street
Butler PA 16001

Just One Restless Rider

Reflections on Trains and Travel

Photographs and Essays by Carlos A. Schwantes

University of Missouri

Columbia and London

387.097
SCH

Copyright © 2009 by

The Curators of the University of Missouri
University of Missouri Press, Columbia, Missouri 65201
Printed and bound in China
All rights reserved
5 4 3 2 1   13 12 11 10 09

Library of Congress Cataloging-in-Publication Data

Schwantes, Carlos A., 1945-
 Just one restless rider : reflections on trains and travel / Carlos A. Schwantes.
    p. cm.
 Includes bibliographical references and index.
 Summary: "A memoir, lavishly illustrated with the author's own photos, of train travel along the legendary rails of America reflecting a lifetime's love of observing and riding trains while tracing the evolution of American passenger trains from the 1950s to the present"—Provided by publisher.
  ISBN 978-0-8262-1859-9 (alk. paper)
  1. Railroad travel—United States—History. 2. Railroads—United States—History. 3. United States—Description and travel. 4. Schwantes, Carlos A., 1945—Travel. I. Title.
  E161.5.S39 2009
  387.0973—dc22   2009009183

♾™ This paper meets the requirements of the American National Standard for Permanence of Paper for Printed Library Materials, Z39.48, 1984.

Design and composition: Jennifer Cropp
Printer and binder: C&C Offset Printing Co., Ltd.
Typefaces: Minion and Return to Earth

Butler Area Public Library
218 North McKean Street
Butler PA 16001

Dedicated to

Ruth Chilcott, Gregory P. Ames, and Edward W. Nolan

Contents

Butler Area Public Library
218 North McKean Street
Butler PA 16001

Butler Area Public Library
218 North McKean Street
Butler PA 16001

Foreword

The Restless Rider Absorbing America and the World

Carlos Schwantes has devoted a lifetime of study and observation to the world of travel and how that world has influenced people, architecture, art, and life on our modern globe. It is a great pleasure for me to see this dean of transportation historians taking a moment in mid-career to create an autobiographical study of the ways in which travel—especially travel by train—has influenced his own life and work. His opinions on the world of travel have been shaped through extraordinary experience and a willingness to experience this world firsthand, actively.

Readers will find this book wistful and nostalgic, loaded with sound historical anecdote, and certainly instructive and timely. Professor Schwantes certainly is not writing a plea for fewer gas-guzzling cars and more steel wheels, but his broad and graceful comparative observations of the world of train, air, water, and automobile travel give some consolation to those bewildered by the past glories of travel and how travel could change in the future.

The St. Louis Mercantile Library Association, where Professor Schwantes holds an endowed research position, was founded in the 1840s by individuals who were deeply interested in transcontinental transportation. The library observed much, and its founders and later supporters helped it grow into one of the largest collections of rail, river, and air transportation history in the nation. The library continues to sponsor exhibitions, publications, programs, research, and fellowships that celebrate the great heritage of transportation history. More recently, this work has reflected greater urgency and relevance as the world grapples with the problem of developing cleaner, more efficient, more comfortable, and hopefully more pleasurable means of travel that can help save our precious environment.

It is with great pride that the collections of images that Carlos Schwantes has presented in these linked portfolios are now part of the St. Louis Mercantile Library at the University of Missouri-St. Louis. They are images of a keen observer made into a sweeping memoir dating from the historian's boyhood along the legendary rails of America and extending to the opportunities he has grasped enthusiastically to consider the world of travel in a global context. Readers are fortunate to have this splendidly penned account of one "absorbed" by the romance of travel.

John Neal Hoover
Director, St. Louis Mercantile Library Association
July 2008

Union Pacific's *Challenger* pulls a special train up the winding
Snake River Valley near King Hill, Idaho, in October 1995.

Butler Area Public Library
218 North McKean Street
Butler PA 16001

Preface

Just One Restless Rider is the result of nearly fifty years of reflecting on trains and travel. I consider myself fortunate to have been the beneficiary of nearly twenty years of free travel aboard the small cruise ships of Lindblad Expeditions and the cruise trains of the American Orient Express. Many photographs presented on the following pages resulted from using those two very different mobile platforms to study the passing landscapes of North America with a camera in my hand.

I am not a professional photographer, I hasten to add, someone who earns his or her living primarily from photography. To be honest, my formal training consisted of a single photography class in high school. But for as long as I can remember, my passion has been to capture life around me with some sort of a camera—initially with my plastic Brownie Hawkeye and then with my father's brick-like Argus C3. It may be fate, but after I started this project I learned that my grandfather, Arnaldo Pedro Schwantes, who ran a small hotel in the spa town of São Lourenço, Brazil, took postcard photographs that he sold on the side. I have seen only one of his postcard images, and I have no idea how or when he made it.

A professional photographer I knew only as Mr. Solomon became friends with my father in central Indiana because both men shared fond memories of growing up in Brazil. Mr. Solomon kindly gave me one of his large studio cameras. The beautifully crafted instrument had been popular with professionals in the early twentieth century, but it lacked a lens and shutter. I needed to buy that vital but expensive mechanism out of my meager monthly allowance, a challenge that was impossible. Besides, studio work for which the massive view camera had been designed held no interest for me, and I was not about to lug it into the field.

So I traded Mr. Solomon's gift camera for a used but considerably smaller Yashica twin-lens reflex model at one of the pawn shops that in the early 1960s lined Washington Street, opposite the Indiana State Capitol. My new possession lacked the gleaming brass knobs and finely polished hardwood of Mr. Solomon's studio camera, and it had but one shutter speed that worked: 1/125th of a second. I could control only the aperture. Not surprisingly, for many years I continued to set every camera I owned to 1/125th of a second and compensate accordingly to obtain proper exposure.

In recent years I have used a variety of digital cameras, but mainly those models featuring fold-out viewing screens that enable me to look down to see the image, as I did for years with my twin-lens reflex, instead of ahead through a tiny eyepiece that I find as visually confining as a ship's porthole. The familiar way of seeing had advantages when it came to stabilizing cameras on a

The view from the dome: the Northern Pacific's *North Coast Limited* enters Minneapolis, Minnesota, on a frigid December morning in 1969 on its journey from Seattle to Chicago.

A view of the dome. Along with photographing trains, I always enjoyed collecting railroad brochures, such as this one issued by the Great Northern Railway in 1959 to advertise its "incomparable" *Empire Builder.* The railroad's premier train linked Chicago with Portland and Seattle by way of scenic Glacier Park.

moving platform, like a boat or train, the motions of which made a tripod impossible to use. A beanbag positioned atop a ship's railing or braced against the edge of a train's open Dutch door worked beautifully for any camera having a fold-out viewing screen. It had the advantage, too, of allowing the photographer to see on the camera's electronic display the track and train ahead without having to lean out of the moving cars and risk an unexpected and potentially dangerous encounter with a locomotive coming the other way.

Ralph Hopkins, a gifted photographer with the Lindblad organization, taught me some of his personal tricks for taking sharp pictures from a moving boat (such as opening the camera aperture as wide as possible and using the highest shutter speed because the depth-of-field was usually of no consideration in such images). From that beginning, I developed techniques of my own that worked reasonably well in the open vestibule of a fast-moving train. Over the years I also ruined cameras by working in the interminable mists of the Alaska panhandle or through exposure to fine dust particles that worked their way into my lenses while photographing from a train.

It is common for historians in the introduction to their books to proclaim something to the effect that "I alone am responsible for any errors of fact or judgment that may occur in the pages that follow." I certainly subscribe to that noble sentiment, but knowing that photographs are an intensely personal aesthetic statement, I add that I hope readers like my images; however, ultimately I alone must take responsibility for what I have chosen to include. I make no apologies for making this book an intensely personal reflection on trains and travel.

Butler Area Public Library
218 North McKean Street
Butler PA 16001

A Norfolk Southern freight train roars through a dilapidated West Virginia coal town on the former Norfolk and Western main line west of Bluefield.

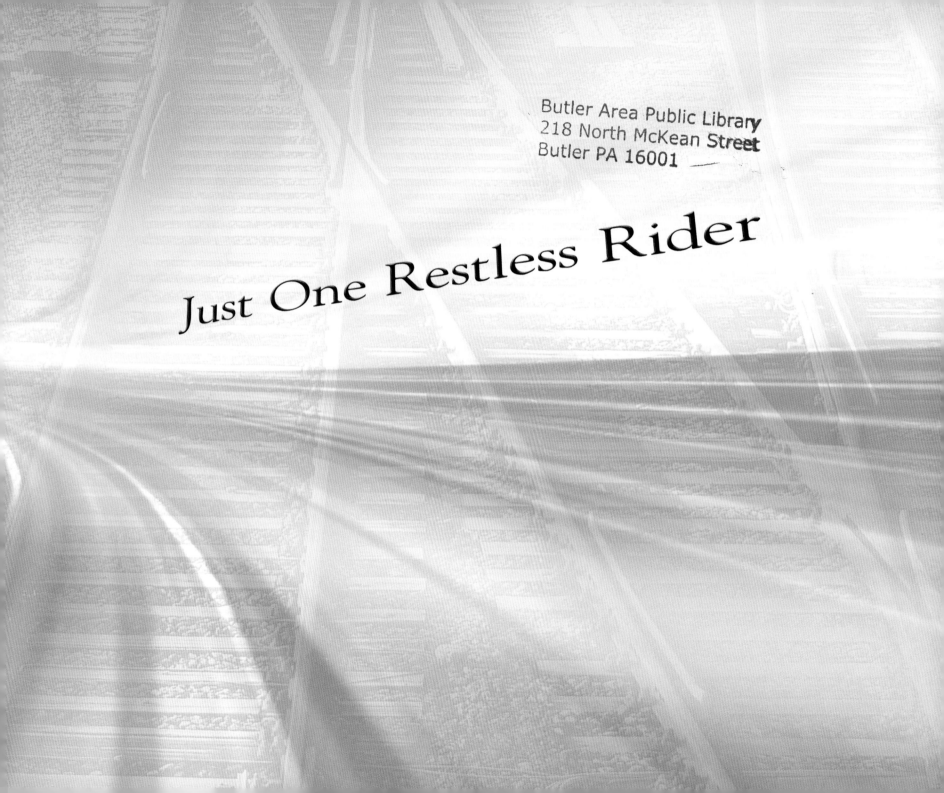

Just One Restless Rider

Butler Area Public Library
218 North McKean Street
Butler PA 16001

Sorting through a box of long-forgotten negatives, I found this picture of a New York Central passenger train speeding toward Indianapolis from Cleveland on a winter day in the early 1960s. At the time the Central ran at least four passenger trains each way along this line, including the *Gateway*, the *Knickerbocker*, and the *Southwestern*, which also served St. Louis. Regrettably, I took no pictures of Pennsy's trains when they ran through my Indiana backyard in the 1950s.

Introduction
Just One Restless Rider

This was a train station. The people here weren't paying attention to much more than their own business. There were trains to meet or catch, baggage to check, meals to eat, cigarettes and magazines to buy, shoes to have shined.

—Jim Lehrer, *Flying Crows*

The train called the *City of New Orleans*, as remembered in the song written by Steve Goodman and transformed into a hit by troubadour Arlo Guthrie, was obviously clanking through its twilight years. As grim as the future was for the Illinois Central train that Goodman proclaimed in 1970 had the "disappearing railroad blues," the nine-hundred-mile journey from Chicago to New Orleans endured by its "restless riders" could have been far worse. And often it was for train travelers in those days. The *City of New Orleans* as Goodman recalled it had fifteen cars, which was exactly fourteen more than made up the *Spirit of St. Louis* that same year when I made the huge mistake of riding it from Indianapolis to New York.

Growing up in the 1950s alongside the Pennsylvania Railroad's double-track main line linking New York and St. Louis, I witnessed an impressive daily parade of streamlined passenger trains race through our town of Greenfield, Indiana. On March 7, 1955, for example (and my tenth birthday), at least five passenger trains would have passed through Greenfield each way. That number would have included the *Indianapolis Limited*, consisting of a string of sleeping cars run between New York, Washington, and the capital of the Hoosier State; *The Allegheny*; *The St. Louisan*; *The American*; and, of course, the flagship *Spirit of St. Louis*. That all-Pullman train was my favorite, and it became the embodiment of my youthful ambition. Standing by the track as a boy, I always hoped that one day I, too, would enjoy the luxury of traveling aboard the *Spirit of St. Louis*, sleeping in one of its posh Pullman cars, and savoring a leisurely dinner in its diner.[1]

Still other passenger trains whooshed past my parents' house each day. One unusually intriguing one was a lengthy train called *The Penn Texas*. In addition to the familiar Tuscan red cars favored by Pennsy management was a rainbow assortment of sleepers belonging to the Missouri Pacific, Frisco, and Missouri-Kansas-Texas, three St. Louis-based railroads that forwarded them in trains serving Oklahoma and Texas. Another named train—and this one I rode several times—was the economy streamliner

1. For further discussion, see my book *Going Places: Transportation Redefines the Twentieth-Century West.*

The brochure cover illustrates how I would like to re-member the railroads of my youth. Coincidentally, this publication dates from 1945, the year of my birth.

called the *Jeffersonian*. Pennsy's all-coach train was intended to meet the basic travel requirements of the average American as idealized by Thomas Jefferson, hence the name. However, to ride the upscale *Spirit of St. Louis* remained my childhood dream.

When our family purchased its first television in the early 1950s, the nearest broadcasting stations were all located in Indianapolis, about twenty miles away, and the black and white pictures that flickered to life across the tiny screen were all rather fuzzy even on the best of days. But whenever one of the Pennsy's many passenger or freight trains bounded past our house it somehow disturbed the weak signals and completely scrambled the picture. Programs like *I Love Lucy* dissolved into electronic snow until the train was gone. I recall that Pennsy's big steam locomotives seemed to cause the worst problems in reception. Of course, if only I had been able to see clearly into the future I would have rushed outside to watch the parade of soon-to-be-discarded steam locomotives and left *I Love Lucy* for the reruns. I vaguely recall, too, that once when a freight train derailed near the center of town a boxcar burst open like a struck piñata filled with toys of all types. Every child, it seems, had an early Christmas present that year thanks to the Pennsylvania Railroad.

As I watched Pennsy trains pass our home in the early to mid-1950s I came to realize that the next train might be pulled either by a diesel or steam locomotive. The order of engines powering the trains seemed entirely random. It was impossible for me to predict. In my youthful mind, that was the way a great railroad worked—and would probably always work. Then one day I heard a train approaching, and I darted out the back screen door to watch it pass. What I saw was wholly unexpected. A very long train composed entirely of steam locomotives, but all without steam, clanked slowly by. Lined up like tired circus elephants, they were on their way to be scrapped. After that I saw no more Pennsy

trains pulled by steam. Such a transformation had seemed inconceivable only months earlier; I had always expected steam locomotives to be around.

The Pennsylvania Railroad was the mightiest thing I knew. The federal government, I was told in school, was much bigger, but as far as I could see it ran only the Greenfield post office. To me a single Pennsy train was more impressive than our town's post office. What I did not know in the 1950s was that my mighty and beloved Pennsy suffered an insidious form of financial hardening of the arteries. The self-proclaimed "Standard Railroad of the World" was no longer the robust enterprise most people still believed it was, nor was its sclerotic management planning well for the future.

I did not recognize the significance of all those heavily loaded semi-trucks grinding through Greenfield along crowded U.S. 40, or of the occasional DC-3 that droned overhead. When I first visited Weir Cook Airport, now Indianapolis International Airport, onlookers could stand at a chain-link fence located only yards from the airplanes and watch the activity. The majestic Super-G Constellations operated by Trans-World Airlines particularly thrilled me, but I also enjoyed the DC-3s favored by regional carriers like Ozark and Lake Central. Watching the Constellations and even the much smaller DC-3s start their big radial engines was high drama for an eleven or twelve-year-old boy. As their pistons roared to life they belched forth impressive clouds of smoke. Even now I can hear their distinctive thunder in my mind. The tall red fire extinguishers wheeled into position close to the engines heightened the sense of drama and reminded me that starting them did not always go as planned. Commercial aviation was exotic, but never could I have imagined that most travelers would soon abandon luxurious trains like the *Spirit of St. Louis* for the DC-3s or even the plush Constellations.

This image from a 1949 brochure advertising the *Broadway Limited* that ran between New York and Chicago also evokes for me memories of the glory days of Pennsylvania Railroad's passenger service between New York and St. Louis in the 1950s.

The jets of Trans-World Airlines connected Indianapolis with New York and other major cities, all without an intervening hub. In the early 1960s the nation's airlines had not yet invented their networks of hubs and spokes. At that time, too, visitors could also wait near the planes for arriving passengers. Life for flyers was so much simpler in those days.

I must add here that my parents took me regularly to church, and the experience inclined me during much of my youth to perceive moral lessons in all that happened in life. That, I later came to realize, was typical of the Seventh-day Adventist worldview, which maintained that the apocalypse could occur at any time and that signs of the coming end were readily visible to any vigilant observer. One indispensable member of our tiny congregation of true believers was a woman I shall call Mary. She was our pianist. I know nothing of Mary's background, other than that she was an African American living in a predominately white community. She never possessed many of the world's material goods. Her tiny house, which my mother and I visited occasionally on Friday evenings, the start of our Sabbath day of worship, did not even have indoor plumbing, which I then concluded was the true dividing line between affluence and poverty.

Mary kept house for a prominent banker's family in Greenfield, as she had apparently done for many years. As a reward for her service, the banker presented Mary with a generous retirement gift to provide for her old age and allow her finally to enjoy some of life's luxuries. He gave her shares, perhaps many shares, of what he thought was one of the safest securities money could buy (a stock for "widows and orphans," as it was popularly phrased) in a company that had paid regular dividends for more than a century, even during the Great Depression of the 1930s. Yes, he based Mary's retirement income, at least in part, on Pennsylvania Railroad common stock. The Pennsylvania and its long-time rival the New York Central merged in 1968, but their marriage was doomed from the start by ongoing institutional incompatibility. Soon the Penn Central paid no more dividends, a sad turn of events that confirmed my belief that there were no guarantees in life. When the nation's largest railroad enterprise went bankrupt in 1970, it was the biggest and most shocking corporate bust in the United States to that time. I have no idea what became of Mary. I could easily guess the outcome, however.

In 1958, well before the Penn Central debacle, our family moved from our trackside rental in Greenfield to a home of our own in suburban Indianapolis. No longer did I watch trains from my backyard (or wonder whether we lived on the right or wrong side of the tracks). A long hike through weeds and woods took me to the New York Central's main line between Indianapolis and Cleveland (the "Big Four Route," as many people in Indiana still recalled it), but at the time I considered the Central to be deprived next of kin to my idealized Pennsy, and so why waste my time and precious money photographing the Central?[2]

That same year, 1958, I discovered copies of *Trains* and *Railroad Magazine* on a rack in the local Haag Drugstore, and I enjoyed reading both publications. Thanks to a kindly ticket agent, I also discovered the most wonderful railroad publication of all, a monthly book nearly two-inches thick bearing the redolent title of *The Official Guide of the Railways and Steam Navigation Lines of the United States, Porto Rico, Canada, Mexico and Cuba*. I could literally hold the domain of the North American railroads on my lap and learn from *Official Guide* maps and timetables the location of individual companies and when and where their trains ran. I used those timetables to launch many make-believe journeys around the United States and Canada, odysseys of the mind that always began in Indianapolis aboard my beloved *Spirit of St. Louis*.

With the help of the *Official Guide* and a good imagination, I traveled through West Virginia coal country aboard the *Poca-*

hontas of the Norfolk and Western, the piney woods of Mississippi aboard the *Gulf Coast Rebel* of the Gulf, Mobile, and Ohio, and to the far-corners of North America aboard countless other trains. I later learned that I could purchase a well-thumbed *Official Guide* from 1943, and in this way I expanded my opportunities chronologically. It was marvelous to learn geography from the ground up. Even now, I have a desire to drive through every county of the United States with my camera and record the vernacular landscape. So far I have done so for all but a dozen of the nation's more than three-thousand counties. But that is a subject for another book.

Years passed, and I left Indiana for college and graduate school in Michigan. In 1969 I began teaching at a small Seventh-day Adventist college in the state of Washington. At the time I had completed only a master's degree in history, but as the bloody war in Vietnam grew increasingly unpopular, I was grateful to be teaching. Only months earlier, President Lyndon Johnson summarily terminated draft deferments for my cohort of graduate students. Fortunately, members of my Indianapolis draft board let me present an appeal in person to remain in school long enough to finish the degree already in progress. Failing that, I was resigned to serving in the Army as an unarmed medic in the jungles of Vietnam or as one of the human guinea pigs in the Army's top-secret germ warfare program ("Operation Whitecoat") at Fort Detrick, near Frederick, Maryland. Those unpleasant alternatives awaited young men whose church leaders had encouraged them to register for the draft and serve in the military but not to carry a weapon of any type.[3]

---

2. The name "Big Four" derived from the Cleveland, Cincinnati, Chicago, and St. Louis Railroad.

3. Talk about being "railroaded" into something unpleasant: "Operation Whitecoat," as best I understood it from college friends who were already in it, involved injecting Army "volunteers" with diluted strains

Butler Area Public Library
218 North McKean Street
Butler PA 16001

Though as a naïve lad of eleven or twelve I didn't believe the New York Central compared favorably to the Pennsylvania, the Central's various publicity pamphlets were just as colorful as the ephemera issued by my favorite railroad.

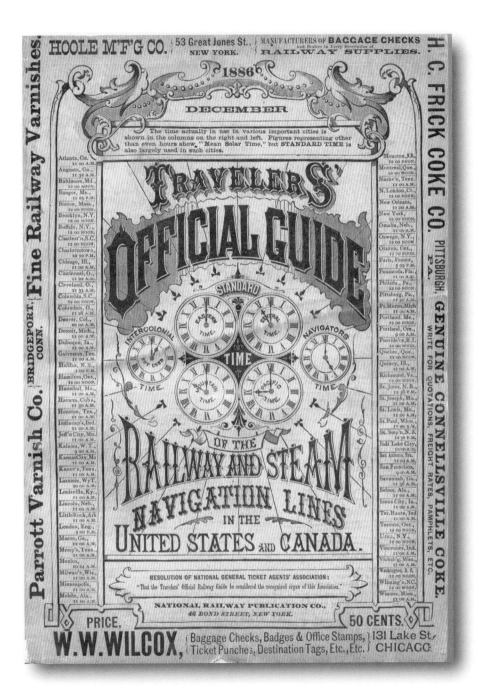

The ornate cover of the *Official Guide* for December 1886. Note the attention it gives to standard time zones to which most railroads of North America had adapted their operations only three years earlier. In the 1950s the *Official Guide* also featured schedules for some of America's major airlines. In addition to acquiring a few copies of *Russell's Official National Motor Coach Guide*, a huge monthly compilation of maps and schedules for the once ubiquitous intercity bus lines of the United States and Canada, I also sought the *Official Airline Guide*, a monthly that featured comprehensive maps and schedules for airlines worldwide. Today the St. Louis Mercantile Library houses a nearly complete set of the monthly *Official Guide of the Railways*. With copies dating back to the early 1870s, this is the world's biggest and best holdings of an invaluable reference tool.

My father had served as an unarmed soldier in World War II, but because he was bilingual in English and Portuguese he ended up being reassigned from the Medical to the Signal Corps to work in Italy as a translator for officers dealing with the allied Brazilian Army. On occasion he traded the cigarettes Uncle Sam issued to all GI's (though he did not smoke) to Italian train crews for the chance to run a steam locomotive. The fighting had ruined the tracks in many places, and thus he was limited in how far he could go, but he enjoyed playing engineer and his Italian mentors were glad for the smokes. The Fifth Army also sent Corporal Schwantes on occasion to Lake Como, which even in the midst of World War II remained an earthly paradise evocative of the Belle Epoch. Frankly, my father had a very good time serving in the Army, and he often said so. I knew I could not possibly fare so well in Vietnam in 1968.

Wearing my best suit, I met with members of my local draft board in a room I still remember as large, cold, and intimidating, but as individuals the board members were extremely warm. One of them urged me to sit down, saying, "Young man, we like your looks. What can we do for you?" Perhaps that was his euphemistic way of saying, "You don't come from the wrong part of Indianapolis," but I naively did not imagine any racial or ethnic overtones at the time. In the end, the board members unanimously encouraged me to find work as a teacher, a job classification that was still draft exempt, and even more amazing, they allowed me six months to search. Honestly, I think my draft board members were no more enthusiastic about the Vietnam War at that time than I was.

With the formal blessing of my draft board, I temporarily dropped out of graduate school and began my lengthy teaching career working as an "Instructor," a position that occupied the very bottom rung of the academic ladder. As befitted my lowly status, my first office at Walla Walla College was not much roomier than a walk-in closet. Along its ceiling ran a myriad of steam pipes that clanged and banged constantly on cold days. The job itself paid less than five thousand dollars a year, a figure low even for a beginner in 1969, but church leaders had classified the meager stipend as a "missionary" wage, implying that the job should entail personal sacrifice for the greater good of the cause. Nonetheless, during the next eighteen months I somehow managed to scrape together enough money to indulge my long-deferred dream of riding aboard the *Spirit of St. Louis.*

The quality of many passenger trains had declined significantly since the late 1950s. In fact, many lines, even entire railroads, had eagerly discontinued passenger service. Most remaining railroads would gladly have followed suit had government regulators granted them permission. To gain what they requested from regulators, who tended to evaluate proposals to discontinue trains by counting the number of riders they served, some railroad companies cunningly did all they could to discourage travelers and drive ridership figures as low as possible. They rid even their best trains of food service and sleeping cars and let the rest of their passenger equipment decay in slow-motion. For some reason I cannot explain now, I believed that the *Spirit of St. Louis* would remain an exception to the noticeable decline in passenger service that Goodman lamented in the *City of New Orleans.*

of deadly diseases to learn how to make Cold War vaccines. One young Adventist, later to become a medical doctor himself, told me he received what was apparently a shot of tularemia microbes ("rabbit fever") followed, ironically, by a pass enabling him to spend the weekend in Washington, D.C. Project White Coat is a well-documented fact, though it sounds like a nightmare conceived by horror writer Stephen King. In all, about 2,300 young Adventists served in "Operation Whitecoat."

The Canadian Pacific's transcontinental *Canadian* paused at Lake Louise station on its way to Vancouver in mid-June 1973. My father is in the tan jacket.

My father (left) and an Army buddy posed somewhere along the tracks in northern Italy during World War II.

The Indianapolis Union Station, where I expected to board the *Spirit of St. Louis* for New York, was an imposing edifice, or so it had been in the 1950s when I enjoyed the streamlined displays that showcased the products of local industry. I recall that Allison, a division of General Motors, featured a model turbo-prop airplane engine that an onlooker could activate by pressing a button. Union Station was where I could sometimes talk a kindly ticket agent out of his outdated copy of the *Official Guide* or raid the rack always well-stocked with timetables and other railroad ephemera—though by my time only the Pennsylvania, New York Central, and Monon railroads still had anything to display. In earlier years the passenger trains of the Baltimore and Ohio, Nickel Plate, and Illinois Central had steamed in and out of Union Station, but no more.

Indianapolis claimed the first union station in the world after it opened to passengers in 1853. The Union Station I knew was a much later construction, an imposing Romanesque structure that dated from 1883. Eighty years later the Indianapolis Union Station remained one of the city's grand edifices in terms of sight and sound and smell. The residual odor of cigar smoke in the men's room, I always liked to imagine, recalled the late 1880s when local Civil War hero, President Benjamin Harrison, boarded the trains here. In 1900 more than two hundred steam trains a day linked Indianapolis with the rest of the world. At the time they all reached the station over street-level tracks, but when I knew the Union Station all its trains ran on bridges and viaducts that carried the tracks safely above the city's busy streets. Thus in the cavernous waiting room the arriving trains announced themselves by their loud rumbling as they passed above the gate area that gave passengers access to the tracks. Uniformed agents swung open the heavy metal gates only at arrival and departure times.

Details from the still imposing façade of the Indianapolis Union Station as I photographed them during the summer of 2008. The edifice is now partially preserved as the centerpiece of a Crowne Plaza Hotel complex.

Train announcements, growing increasingly unintelligible as an electronically amplified nasal voice echoed from wall to wall of the huge waiting room, added to the sensual experience of this young observer. The announcer would say something like, "Pennsylvania Railroad train number four, *The Penn Texas*, is now departing for [unintelligible], Columbus, Pittsburgh [unintelligible], Altoona, [more unintelligible station stops], and New York City."

From the moment I entered the chillingly empty building in late December 1970 I sensed that the patron saint of high-quality passenger train service had long-ago fled the Indianapolis Union Station for some unintelligible destination. Even then, however, I remained in denial. I still looked forward to boarding the *Spirit of St. Louis* for New York, where I would change to one of the New Haven trains bound for Boston, site of that year's annual conference of the American Historical Association. As I recall, I even indulged by purchasing a ticket for one of the New Haven's parlor cars, a term that had long been synonymous with daytime travel comfort.

The first disconcerting thing I noticed in the Indianapolis Union Station was that the display cases were gone. Perhaps they had been moved to the local airport, which I later discovered was also the fate of many murals once displayed at Cincinnati's art deco Union Station. I saw, too, that large portions of the worse-for-wear Indianapolis station had been boarded up. The portentous rumble of the arriving train was less impressive than I remembered it in the 1950s, and soon I learned why; the once-great *Spirit of St. Louis* had atrophied to a diesel locomotive and one coach to accommodate the brave (or maybe unwitting) riders. Where's the rest of the train? For an instant I thought that crewmen had divided the train in order to add more cars. But before I had time to look around, the conductor shouted his famil-

iar "All Aboard!" I hurried up the vestibule steps into the greatly overheated coach. No more cars were added that night. The single coach proved more than adequate to accommodate passengers, who at any given time seldom numbered more than fifteen. How restless those riders were, I did not know.

Because it was already dark by the time we pulled out of Indianapolis and passengers had no place to sleep apart from their seats, the conductor dimmed the car lights. At each stop, however, he returned the lights to their brightest possible setting. Was he being safety conscious or spiteful in order to annoy and discourage passengers, thus allowing the Pennsy to convince federal regulators to permit it to drop this woebegone scrap of a once-grand express?

My night was not only sleepless but also foodless. But worse was yet to come. A child sleeping on a seat by the window and above a steam baseboard heater overflowed its already soaked diaper, and soon the distinctive smell of warm urine added to the oppressive atmosphere.

As for through passengers, and I was probably the only glutton for such self-inflicted punishment, we reached New York's Pennsylvania Station in time to connect with the New Haven's Boston-bound train. Settling into my parlor car seat, the first thing I noticed was the massive sheet of plywood that substituted for my window pane. I had looked forward to seeing winter's beauty on display along the New Haven's shoreline route through Connecticut and Rhode Island, but this was an unexpected setback. As I scanned the car for a seat with a clear vista, I noticed that many additional windows had been replaced by sheets of plywood and not one of the remaining glass panes was clean enough to see through.

That did it. I myself now became a thoroughly restless rider eager to get to Boston, cancel the return half of my rail ticket, and

Not so long ago: introduced in the late 1940s, the General Motors' *Train of Tomorrow* anticipated a bright future for America's passenger-carrying railroads in the coming decades.

Butler Area Public Library
218 North McKean Street
Butler PA 16001

A New Haven brochure advertised the railroad's scenic route along the Connecticut shoreline.

book a flight back on American Airlines. Not before or since have I canceled a trip by train. In recent years I have endured grim rides on the trains of Eastern Europe, but during the months before the coming of Amtrak on May 1, 1971, many passenger trains in America had degenerated into rolling nightmares that I had no desire to experience. Conditions aboard the *City of New Orleans* as described in Goodman's song looked almost appealingly superior by comparison.

My first train ride I do not remember at all. My mother tells me that it was in a drawing-room sleeper between Wilmington, North Carolina, and Washington, D.C. My great aunt paid the extra money required to purchase the top luxury accommodation, and if my grandmother behaved true to form she packed a hearty and healthy lunch in a small travel case that for years afterward smelled of bananas. The sleeping car ran on the tracks of the Atlantic Coast Line, a railroad headquartered in Wilmington, as it had been for more than a century. My grandfather, great-grandfather, and great-great-grandfather had all worked for the Coast Line.

My great-great-grandfather, John Casteen, joined the Wilmington and Weldon Railroad shortly after the Civil War. He had spent the last months of the conflict in the Elmira, New York, prison camp into which the Union stuffed its captured Confederates. "Hellmira," some prisoners called it because of the cramped conditions. John Casteen, upon release, apparently concluded that if the South's cause was lost, then the best thing for an ambitious young man was to work for the railroads that were rapidly binding the broken nation together again. I wonder if a loyal member of the First North Carolina infantry, a Rebel obviously passionate in his support for secession, ever pondered the irony. As far as I know John Casteen left no personal records of any type.

Perhaps he was not even literate. All I have are a dozen pages copied from Civil War records at the National Archives. Those documents note dryly that as a member of Robert E. Lee's Army of Northern Virginia, John Casteen participated in numerous battles (including both Antietam and Gettysburg), endured a long and difficult recuperation from battlefield dysentery in Chimborazo Hospital in Richmond, and became a Northern prisoner of war on May 12, 1864, at "Bloody Angle" during the fiercely contested Battle of Spotsylvania Court House.

It made sense for him to go to work for the railroad because Wilmington was fast becoming a major railroad town. It formed a transportation hub for lines running north to Norfolk and Petersburg, west to Charlotte, and south to Atlanta. A short distance east of Wilmington was the Atlantic Ocean, which allowed ships steaming along the Cape Fear River to link Wilmington with the great ports of the world. By the 1950s most of those rail spokes belonged to the Atlantic Coast Line. Neighbors living on opposite sides of my grandparents had both retired from the Coast Line, as the railroad was familiarly known. On sultry summer evenings in an era before home air conditioning, neighbors often gathered on a front porch swing and in rocking chairs to swap gossip and stories. I especially enjoy hearing about my grandfather's railroading days. He was a skilled storyteller, and many of his recollections may actually have been true, though I think he was prone to embellish his tales to enhance their humorous effect. The gales of laughter did help to take our minds off the torment of heat and humidity. Perhaps I first developed my life-long interest in history as a result of listening to stories told on my grandparents' porch on Dock Street.

There was, however, one story my grandfather Charles Casteen repeated only with the greatest reluctance, and only when my grandmother goaded him. That one involved the time he walked

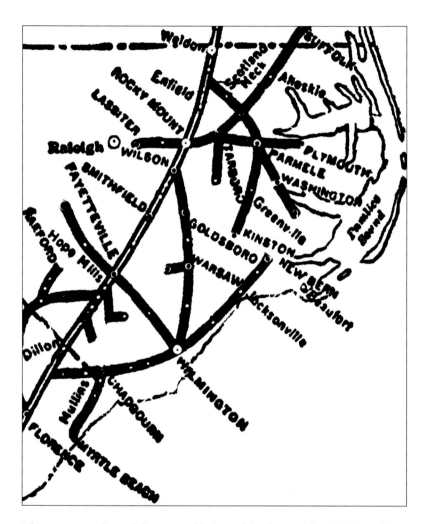

This map as adapted from an old timetable shows Atlantic Coast Line tracks serving the Wilmington, North Carolina, area at the time I was focusing my camera on its trains.

off his job at the Coast Line along with his union brothers during the great shopmen's strike of 1922. The walkout ended the Casteen family's railroading legacy because the companies eventually broke the strike and the union. No longer would my grandfather operate the imposing steam crane the Coast Line used to lift cars back onto its tracks after a derailment. When my grandmother told her version of the great shopmen's strike, it was perhaps with a trace of bitterness in her voice, because even in the 1950s she still seemed to mourn the loss of "C. H.'s" free pass and their chance to travel around the United States by train. She never went west of Indiana, and she traveled that far only by buying herself a ticket.

Dock Street in Wilmington was for me a repository of many pleasant memories, and not just because of the stories told on my grandparents' porch. If I walked downtown for fifteen blocks, past some of the city's remaining antebellum mansions, I ended up at one of the docks lining the broad Cape Fear River. Ancient wooden planks and massive pilings smelled of creosote preservative on hot days—and summer days in Wilmington were invariably hot. Temporary relief arrived with the afternoon thunderstorms, although following their sound and fury and brief torrential downpours, the streets of Wilmington were even more humid and its wooden docks more pungent.

I only remember him as Captain Varnam. He piloted one of the fire-engine red tugboats that tied up near the foot of Dock Street. Occasionally he took pity on the fourteen-year-old boy who hung around the waterfront with his Brownie camera. Whether or not company rules permitted it, he offered me rides downriver to the North Carolina state docks to move an oceangoing ship. Some of my first grainy black and white pictures were of tugboats and Wilmington's working waterfront. Apparently it never occurred to me to take a picture of Captain Varnam.

One of my early pictures of oceangoing ships on the Cape Fear River that defined the Wilmington waterfront. I always did favor a romantic picture in the soft-focus style of the "pictorialist" photographers who flourished at the beginning of the twentieth century.

Later I learned that my great-great-uncle, Zeb Hodges (named for Zebulon Vance, North Carolina's popular Civil War governor), had worked as a young clerk in one of the big warehouses that lined the waterfront. The buildings through which passed cargoes of fish fertilizer, turpentine, and other products essential to the economy of coastal Carolina in Uncle Zeb's day have either been demolished or gentrified into upscale boutiques and pricy restaurants. The Wilmington waterfront has lost the gritty charm that captivated me as a teenager, and today it swarms with tourists.

Uncle Zeb once gave me an intricately detailed wooden tugboat he built from scratch, probably during the lulls when no cargoes passed through the warehouse for him to tally. The model, about the size of a football and painted a brilliant shade of red, was a wonder to admire, but I made the mistake of attempting to sail it across my grandparents' bathtub one muggy summer afternoon. Uncle Zeb's handicraft unexpectedly turned turtle, and I watched in dismay as all its rigging floated loose in the water. Despite his gift of the boat model, I think it fair to describe Uncle Zeb as a somewhat miserly old man. He lived in a large house behind my grandparents' more modest one, and, in fact, he had squirreled away enough money to own both houses and many more rentals.

He would pay me a few pennies to climb high in his backyard fig tree and pick a bucket of the sweet purple fruit before the crows and other birds could eat it all. The fig leaves were intolerably scratchy, and that made me wonder whether Adam and Eve ever really wore clothes made from such uncomfortable material. Uncle Zeb's fig tree may have been the beginning of my downward slide in religious belief, for in those days I had an excessively literal interpretation of all things Biblical. Moreover, I have never since then liked the cloying taste of figs.

Another of my photographs of activity at the North Carolina state docks in Wilmington. The time was the late 1950s or early 1960s.

Uncle Zeb married for the first time only at the age of sixty-five. He once confided to me in his low, gravely voice that he enjoyed marriage well enough that he should have considered it ten years sooner. I often visited with Uncle Zeb in his porch swing, prodding him to tell me stories about Wilmington "in the old days." With each passing summer, however, he seemed to remember fewer and fewer stories. In his last years as he grew progressively more senile, his long-standing enthusiasm to work with concrete reached truly bizarre proportions as he constructed concrete gutters everywhere he could imagine water running through the yards during one of Wilmington's afternoon downpours. My grandmother, who from her kitchen window could

My mother or grandmother snapped this picture of Uncle Zeb and me preparing concrete for another of his great canalization projects, this one dating from the late 1940s.

see him shuffling across the yard with his ancient wheelbarrow and fresh sacks of cement, would invariably exclaim in exasperation, "Oh no, here comes uncle again!"

Uncle Zeb's gutters fascinated me because over time his handiwork resembled a network of miniature canals. With the aid of a garden hose I could float toy boats from my grandparents' back yard to uncle's garage next door. Growing tired of my maritime adventure, I could usually borrow uncle's well-used wheelbarrow and other construction equipment and fashion an assemblage that resembled a passenger train. The Koester boys, who lived close by on Dock Street, usually made willing passengers. In those innocent days I could imagine nothing more interesting than trains, boats, planes, and automobiles. Naïve me!

When I grew old enough to take my camera to the Cape Fear docks, I wandered far enough along the waterfront and up Front Street to Wilmington's Coast Line station. Wilmington had two passenger train stations and one bus station. The big intercity motor coaches operated by Atlantic Greyhound, Carolina Trailways, and the Seashore Transportation Company interested me almost as much as the Coast Line's passenger trains. On several occasions my mother and I rode an intercity bus from Wilmington to Washington, D.C., to see Uncle Charles and Aunt Barbara before we boarded one of the Pennsy's trains to continue our end-of-summer journey home to Indianapolis.

The Wilmington bus station once had three waiting rooms, one for white passengers, another for "colored" passengers traveling within the state of North Carolina, and a third for travelers of color headed to destinations in other states. This odd racial arrangement was something a boy who spent most of the year in Indiana found puzzling. In my grandfather's small personal library I once found a book compiling the laws of Wilmington, which he was supposed to enforce as the city's chief of police in

Passenger trains in Wilmington's Atlantic Coast Line Station in the late 1950s.

the early 1940s. One segregation law, as I recall it, required that bowling alley operators maintain a wall at least six feet high between lanes used by white and black patrons. Apparently it was like the dividers, often only painted stripes or flimsy curtains, that segregated black and white riders aboard trains and buses of the Old South.

One of my many cousins in Wilmington was Thurston Davis, a young man just a few years older than I, who occasionally worked as a ticket agent at the Wilmington bus station. Sometimes I could talk him out of an outdated copy of *Russell's Guide*, the bus equivalent to the *Official Guide of the Railways*. I did not know Thurston or most of my other southern cousins well, but years ago I somehow came to believe that this young man had his head fatally rearranged when he jumped up just as his brother pulled the trigger of a shotgun during a hunting outing together. During a recent visit with another cousin in Wilmington, I learned to my great relief that Thurston was alive and well, but for years

that gory tale had been real enough to me. I have come to realize that cheerless stories, often the essence of today's country music, formed an integral part of the painful mental baggage every true southerner carried around in those days, and that baggage usually included a few ghost stories as well. Pain and laughter seemed but two sides of the same historical coin.

The imposing Atlantic Coast Line station in Wilmington was supposed to have been a greatly modified version of the Washington, D.C., Union Station. Perhaps that was true, but I never could see a resemblance. It was, nonetheless, a building that housed the railroad's corporate headquarters on several floors stacked above the main passenger waiting area. Years earlier, Wilmington was located on the railroad's main line, but the Atlantic Coast Line completed a shortcut through Fayetteville in the early 1890s. After that time most through traffic traveled the new way, including the luxurious New York-Florida trains of the 1920s, one of which

Another of my vintage pictures taken in Wilmington's Atlantic Coast Line Station in the late 1950s or early 1960s. The waiting trains connected Wilmington to the railroad's main line at Rocky Mount, North Carolina, and Atlanta, Georgia.

the Florida East Coast ran island-hopping on its "oversea" line all the way to Key West, just ninety miles from the sensuous pleasures of Havana.

In the 1950s many of the Coast Line's best trains bore some variation of the name "Champion" and were pulled by modern diesel locomotives painted a sporty purple. The train names and the unusual color were supposedly favorites of the railroad's long-time president, a man most people in Wilmington called "Champ" Davis. His full and proper name was actually Champion McDowell Davis.

The Coast Line's Wilmington passenger trains ran north to Washington, D.C. (actually only to the junction town of Rocky Mount, North Carolina, except for through Pullman cars), and southwest to Atlanta. Both trains included sleepers in their make-up. An elderly black man cleaned the cars during their turnaround in the Wilmington station. On one occasion he allowed me to check them out inside but warned that I had better be careful where I walked because electricity would pool up in some areas of the floor. I always wondered if this was his sly way of teasing me.

The Seaboard Airline Railroad had a much less imposing station consisting of little more than a waiting room tucked into one corner of a brick warehouse, as I recall, and the only passenger train on its Wilmington branch shuffled back and forth to Charlotte. Apparently most travelers in the area drove cars or rode the red-striped buses of Queen City Trailways because not many passengers still traveled on the Seaboard's road-weary train in the late 1950s. It seldom amounted to more than a diesel locomotive and two or three hand-me-down baggage cars and a coach. The Koester boys, all four of them, once rode the Seaboard train to Acme, a lowly stop about ten miles west of Wilmington, to see their grandparents. That awed me, and for days after they returned home, every time I saw Carl or Dickey I asked him to tell me about their journey on the Seaboard. In

The Seaboard's passenger train in Wilmington in the late 1950s. Daily it plodded between Wilmington and Charlotte, a distance of 190 miles, at an average speed of just twenty-five miles-per-hour, and that was on the longest stretch of straight track in the United States. No wonder it had few riders and ceased running soon after I took this picture.

those days the main claim to fame of the Seaboard's Wilmington branch was that it contained the longest stretch of straight track in the United States.

On the other hand, the Coast Line branch into Wilmington from Florence and Atlanta could claim Joe Baldwin's ghost. Many residents of North Carolina have their favorite ghost stories, and some of them, including the Joe Baldwin tale, have become chapters in book-length compilations.[4] Joe Baldwin, so one of many variations of this ghost story goes, worked as a conductor (or

4. For example, see the Joe Baldwin story in Nancy Roberts, *North Carolina Ghosts and Legends* (Columbia: University of South Carolina Press, 1991 reprint of 1959 edition): 97-100.

As this picture from the late 1950s illustrates, the Seaboard local between Wilmington and Charlotte provided but a single coach to accommodate passengers, which was probably more than enough space.

maybe brakeman) for the Wilmington and Manchester Railroad. Brakemen did the most dangerous work on any railroad until the carriers added air brakes and knuckle couplers to their cars in the late nineteenth century. One dark night in the spring of 1867 (or possibly 1856, according to another version) the last car of Baldwin's Wilmington-bound train accidentally separated from the rest at Maco station in a swampy area about fourteen miles west of the Cape Fear River. Despite Joe's desperate signaling with his oil lantern, the following train plowed into the stopped one. As the cars slammed together they decapitated the unfortunate man. For years Joe was supposed to walk along the track on dark nights, swinging his lantern to and fro as he searched for his missing head.

Life Magazine ran a story about Joe Baldwin and the mysterious Maco light in 1957. Though at a rational level I did not believe in ghosts, the possibility of viewing with my own eyes the mysterious swinging lantern along the right-of-way so intrigued me that I persuaded Mickey Koseruba to borrow his parents' car and take us to the spot where the accident supposedly occurred. I

soon discovered that a moonless night in a swamp made me uneasy. Was the splash I heard merely the sound of a nervous frog, or was a water moccasin or alligator eyeing me in the blackness? For certain, Mickey and I could not distinguish between the unearthly glow of Baldwin's swinging lantern and the headlights of cars occasionally passing along a nearby highway.

In 1967 the Coast Line and Seaboard merged, and today they form part of the CSX Corporation, at least what is left of their original rail lines. A map of CSX's present sprawling system suggests that the railroad has removed much track belonging to the former Coast Line and Seaboard railroads in the Wilmington area. The section of track supposedly frequented by the lantern-swinging Baldwin came up in 1977. I have no idea if old Joe stills haunts the former right-of-way. I am inclined to believe that the strange lights observers claimed to have seen along the tracks all those years amounted to little more than luminous puffs of swamp gas. True believers in the legend will never agree with me.

For obvious reasons I have no pictures of Joe Baldwin's light. In fact, after my box-camera outings in Wilmington as a teenager I took no more pictures of trains for many years. Despite my photography class at Broad Ripple High School in Indianapolis, I never considered using my camera and darkroom skills in a serious way. Not until after I relocated from Walla Walla College to the University of Idaho in Moscow in 1984 did my interest in railroad photography revive for the long-term. At first my intent was only to record what remained of railroad service in the Moscow area.

The Union Pacific and Burlington Northern tracks through the rolling Palouse wheat country surrounding Moscow seemed to be used less and less frequently. One week the former Northern Pacific track running east from Moscow to Troy and down a

The Union Pacific switching cars in Moscow, Idaho, in September 1986. Grain elevators defined the background in a railroad landscape now changed forever. Twelve years later a popular bicycle trail replaced Union Pacific tracks along the eight miles that separated the communities of Moscow and Pullman, home, respectively, to the University of Idaho and Washington State University.

winding grade to Lewiston was intact, and the next week it was gone. I wondered what track might be removed next. Today's Bill Chipman bicycle trail that skirts the main highway linking Moscow and Pullman, Washington, was once Union Pacific track. As it turned out, both railroads had abandoned or sold off their branch lines in the region by the time I moved to St. Louis in 2001. I only wish I had found more time to record their twilight years in scenic Palouse Country.

In another way, though, I was incredibly lucky. One day in 1990 I received a phone call from New York. The woman on the other end of the line asked if I would like to serve as a tour lecturer for Sven-Olaf Lindblad's Special Expeditions' cruise boats on the Columbia River. She had heard from a colleague at Gonzaga University that I often taught week-long field classes on the explorers Lewis and Clark for the University of Idaho's summer school program. Frankly, at that time I knew nothing about the Lindblad organization, and so I deferred my decision, telling Pamela Fingleton that I would call her back the next day with an answer. Almost immediately I phoned my travel agent and asked her about the company. "Oh, they're the Mercedes-Benz of tour companies," was her reply. That was good enough, and so for nearly twenty years I worked a week here and there as a naturalist/ historian for Lindblad Expeditions aboard its vessels cruising the Columbia River, Alaska's Inside Passage, and the Mediterranean Sea.

On board the vessels now known as the *National Geographic Sea Lion* or *National Geographic Sea Bird* I observed and photographed all types of transportation. Lengthy Union Pacific freight trains thundered along the south bank of the Columbia River, while those of Burlington Northern Santa Fe followed the north bank. In addition, various barge lines hauled grain, frozen French fries, wood chips, and often petroleum and fertilizer along the Great River of the West. As muscular towboats bucked currents and winds, the spray made an impressive sight.

In 1995 I received another unexpected phone call, this time from a travel agency that at the time operated the *American Orient Express* cruise train. It seemed that a copy of my new book, *Railroad Signatures Across the Pacific Northwest* (1993), showcasing many eye-catching illustrations of trains (but with only one photo taken by its author, I must add) had impressed someone within the company. Would I like to travel with the *American Orient Express* as a lecturer? Another dream had come true. To cruise free around the United States, Canada, and Mexico enjoying the amenities of a luxury train was a thrill beyond my wildest imagination.

Between 1995 and 2008, when I retired from the AOE's successor company, GrandLuxe Rail, I rode tens of thousands of miles on more than thirty separate train cruises. Along the way I wore out two or three cameras taking pictures from the open vestibules. Fine dust invariably worked its way into my lenses, though I didn't really mind having to replace cameras occasionally because AOE officials were relaxed about my taking pictures through the open upper-half of the Dutch doors.

Particularly after the terrorist attack on the World Trade Center in 2001, the opportunity to take photographs of the railroad landscape from the open vestibules of the *American Orient Express* proved invaluable. That was because after 9–11 the railroad police became exceedingly skittish about having strangers taking pictures of their trains or support structures. However, working from the cars of the AOE I never had anyone question my intentions or prevent my taking pictures of the railroad landscape. And so I rode back and forth across North America standing at the train's Dutch doors with my camera ready for anything that came along. Had I attempted to do the same

The glamorous *American Orient Express* in Denver's Union Station. This image comes from my first trip aboard the train in the fall of 1995. That year the cruise train traveled between Sacramento, California, and Washington, D.C., by way of Salt Lake City, Denver, Chicago, St. Louis, Indianapolis, Cincinnati, and Charlottesville, a circuitous route that it never used again. In subsequent years it usually crossed the United States by way of New Orleans.

Elegant meals served in one of the train's two dining cars were
among the pleasures of riding the *American Orient Express*.

thing aboard an Amtrak train, I would certainly have incurred the wrath of the conductor.

Traveling aboard an Amtrak train from Montreal to New York City in 1997, I witnessed perhaps the most spectacular sunset of my life as we rolled along the Hudson River Valley south of Albany. Nature's sublime display of light and color was worthy of being captured on film or canvas (as Thomas Cole and like-minded artists of the Hudson River School did in the nineteenth century)—but rather than photograph it through the train's sealed and tinted windows or risk sneaking around the vestibule to open a window and trying the patience of the conductor, I chose to preserve the luminous scene in memory alone.

Shortly after I moved to St. Louis to teach at the University of Missouri, I consciously sought to broaden my horizons by making frequent trips overseas, starting with a journey to Great Britain. A few years earlier, in 1994, the government of Margaret Thatcher had privatized the passenger operations of British Rail by turning train-running over to twenty-six different contract carriers. This presented a tempting opportunity. For years I had collected Amtrak timetables for the United States and VIA Rail timetables for Canada, but I was too young to benefit from the earlier era during which station timetable racks bulged with free folders and brochures for many different railroads.

In Britain, I rediscovered some of that variety in the timetables issued by Virgin Trains, Great North Eastern Railway, First Great Western, and numerous other operating companies. With a first-class Britrail pass I could travel by train whenever and wherever the spirit moved me. During the summer of 2001 I wandered and wondered across much of England, Scotland, and Wales—from London to Penzance, Inverness, and Cardiff, and to a good many other stops of interest along the way. Once when aboard a fast-running Virgin Train from London to Liverpool I briefly experienced a powerful sense of déjà vu, imagining that I was once again speeding across the green heartland of Ohio and Indiana. The attractive car interiors and company color scheme favored by Virgin Trains (vaguely reminiscent of Tuscan Red) recalled to my mind the best streamliners of the Pennsylvania in the 1950s.

After Great Britain—as my travel and language confidence increased—I used a variety of Eurail Passes to venture into increasingly remote parts of the continent, even to Serbia, Bulgaria, and Romania, where train riding could often be an adventure. During July 2007 on an excruciatingly slow ride from Belgrade to Sofia, a couple of cigarette smugglers wedged themselves among the six passengers in our already overly crowded compartment just before we reached the Bulgarian border. The stout women, it turned out later, had stuffed their undergarments with boxes of cheap Serbian smokes they intended to sell on the streets of Sofia.

Their illegal arrangement was as yet a mystery to me as I watched a Bulgarian border inspector randomly poke a screwdriver-like tool through ventilation holes in the compartment ceiling. I could not imagine what he was searching for until later I saw the two heavy-set women return from the restroom—except that now they were physically much smaller. Only then did I realize what had happened. When at long last we reached the Sofia station, they carried their cigarettes triumphantly into the night.

In Eastern Europe traces of a Cold War mindset survived in the officious way some border inspectors checked and stamped passports. Yet, ironically, the politest border official I have ever encountered was while traveling by train from Hungary into Serbia, a country the United States and its NATO allies had bombed in the late 1990s. Initially, I felt a great sense of unease as we approached the checkpoint. However, as the neatly dressed guard handed back my stamped passport, he smiled and

The rising sun burnishes the complex railway landscape leading into Munich's Hauptbahnhof.

added in perfect English, "Welcome to Serbia, Mr. Schwantes. I hope you will enjoy your stay." I did not expect such a courteous welcome. It occurred to me as we rolled toward Belgrade that agreeable surprises such as that made leisure travel enjoyably unpredictable. I recalled the thrill of walking the narrow, winding streets of Venice for the first time and being awestruck by the surprises that awaited me around each corner.

In truth, I cannot get enough of train travel in Europe. The large stations are always a great source of wonderment. Not only are they architecturally fascinating, but in almost all of them the tracks and trains are far more accessible than in their American counterparts. It is not uncommon to see travelers eating snacks on platforms adjacent to trains coming and going, and some of the smaller stations feature outdoor cafes right next to the busy tracks. That arrangement is any train watcher's dream. No wonder I feel a thrill traveling across Europe not unlike that of a ten-year-old on a visit to Disneyland.

Among my all-time favorite stations in Europe is Oriente in suburban Lisbon, Portugal. This station was designed by Santiago Calatrava for the World Expo of 1998 and consciously constructed to embody many design features of a medieval cathedral. Closer to home, Theodore Link, the architect of the magnificent Union Station in St. Louis, the largest such facility in the United States when it opened in 1894, borrowed design elements from the charming medieval town of Carcassone in southern France. In the portfolios that follow, I have photographs that clearly support the assertion that many an imposing railroad station is in truth a "cathedral of commerce."

As I look back, I feel fortunate for what I have experienced during my years of trains and travel. Not only did our rented Greenfield house of the 1950s provide a front row seat from which to observe the railroad industry during its transition from steam to diesel, but it was also located just a block off U.S. 40, the highway corridor that in earlier years had served as America's National Road from Cumberland, Maryland, to Vandalia, Illinois. In our sixth-grade class in Indiana history we learned how pioneers arranged logs in the muddy spots to form the aptly named "corduroy road."

Along Highway 40 I could also see remnants of the old electric interurban line that once linked Indianapolis and Dayton, Ohio. That line, the Terre Haute, Indianapolis, and Eastern, abandoned all train service through Greenfield some fifteen years before we moved there in 1947, but gradually I learned to recognize tell-tale remnants of the former interurban line as I walked through town to school. Sometimes in the early 1950s my mother would take me to Indianapolis on a Central Swallow bus for a day of shopping in the big downtown department stores. In the cavernous Indianapolis bus station I could still see rails shining through the hot asphalt. The building had once been the hub of the most extensive system of electric interurban lines in the United States. It was difficult for me to grasp in the 1950s that early in the century some four-hundred interurban cars had arrived and departed from that station every day.

Offering other fascinating reminders of the past, like those rail remnants in the Indianapolis bus station, were old travel brochures. Over the years I became increasingly fascinated by such ephemera, a word that may puzzle readers not already familiar with it. The nature of ephemera is that it is intended to be used and then thrown away, such as would normally have been the fate of Esso road maps at the conclusion to our family's annual vacation trek from Indiana to North Carolina. My challenge on those road trips was to persuade my long-suffering father to fill our family's big Hudson automobile at a different

The cathedral-like Oriente Station in suburban Lisbon, Portugal, is my personal favorite because of the structure's architectural imagination.

gasoline station each time so that I could collect their free maps. It mattered not that I already had Esso maps for North Carolina and Virginia; I also wanted maps from the display racks of Sunoco, Atlantic, and Gulf stations.

I promised Dad that if he would help me out, I would be his navigator, a job that would keep me from fighting with my younger brother, Dave, in the back seat. My father was not always happy with my directions because I had a bad habit of routing him the long way around so that I could see a stretch of highway new to me. My father, on the other hand, preferred the most direct and most familiar routes, and he wanted to travel along interstate highways, if at all possible. That was not my preference, however. I thought the new interstates boring. To this day, I still prefer a leisurely drive along the secondary roads that have become known as the "Blue Highways."[5]

In more recent years, I have brought back to St. Louis suitcases bulging with timetables and travel brochures from Europe. My intention was to donate them to the St. Louis Mercantile Library to benefit future researchers, though who can really say what use anyone may make of them a hundred years from now? Fortunately, that is not for me to decide. My primary motivation is the realization that today's travel brochures are free for the taking, while yesterday's ephemera, at least the material that has survived, often sells on eBay for dozens of dollars. I much prefer free.

Speaking of ephemera, it was the subject of yet another unexpected phone call, this time leading me to William J. Dixon, retired president of the Chicago, Rock Island, and Pacific Railroad (celebrated in song as a "mighty fine line"). Dixon, I soon learned, was one of the rare corporate executives who was truly

5. The term comes from William Least Heat-Moon, *Blue Highways: A Journey into America* (Boston: Little, Brown and Company, 1983).

The cover of an Esso map for 1972 recalls when the basic standard of service across the United States included free road maps and personal car-care by a uniformed attendant.

passionate about the history of his industry. As improbable as it sounds, his daughter in Seattle had learned from a friend about a man who rented her parent's home twenty years ago during a post-doctoral sabbatical at the University of Washington and had been very interested in the history of railroads. With the skill of a seasoned detective, Dixon's daughter, Angie, tracked me to a St. Louis phone number in 2002. She asked if I would care to visit her father, who had retired from Chicago to Florida along with his large collection of maps, brochures, and postcards. I did, and her father proved to be a charming gentleman and an avid collector of ephemera pertaining to all facets of railroad history. I include more on Bill Dixon and his collection in the final portfolio, which deals with personal perspectives to be gained from utilizing railroad and other travel ephemera in my work as historian.

This personal account summarizes my evolving interest in photographing and studying various forms of transportation. I attempt to share my passion in greater detail in the portfolio introductions and illustration captions that follow. Ideally, all of the introductions to the image portfolios should be roughly similar in length, but I cannot always make the words and observations fit the template. Nonetheless, may you find pleasure in this unhurried and sometimes quirky personal odyssey and not be merely a restless reader.

Butler Area Public Library
218 North McKean Street
Butler PA 16001

The majesty of a steam locomotive running fast: I photographed this
Union Pacific special train near Orchard, Idaho, in October 1995.

Portfolio 1
Not So Long Ago

My early pictures of railroads tend to have been taken sporadically. Regrettably, enormous gaps separate my childhood photos taken in Wilmington, North Carolina, from more serious efforts that date mainly from the early 1990s. Once in a while, however, during the thirteen years I taught at Walla Walla College I did set aside teaching and research responsibilities and escaped to the nearby Blue Mountains of Oregon to spend a relaxing day photographing trains. Mostly, though, I just wrote about them. I sent a few of my general interest essays on local railroad history to the Walla Walla *Union-Bulletin*, which published them in the early 1970s. My newspaper articles resulted in some pleasant but wholly unintended consequences. My original purpose had been simply to inform myself (and any interested readers) about local history, a method of personal inquiry I have used wherever I lived.

Somehow my *Union-Bulletin* articles reached Union Pacific offices at the railroad's headquarters in Omaha. One day I received an unexpected call asking if I would like to ride aboard a special train pulled by Union Pacific steam locomotive 8444 (now 844) on its way to the Spokane World's Fair of 1974. The locomotive giant would form the centerpiece of the Union Pacific exhibit. My ride was from Baker to Pendleton, Oregon, which proved to be a good choice. From Baker to LaGrande the locomotive sped along generally straight and level track, while from LaGrande to Pendleton it slowed to a steady puffing climb to the crest of the Blue Mountains along a serpentine stretch of track that had some of the tightest curves and steepest grades on the Union Pacific.

American railroads in the late 1960s and early 1970s had few steam locomotives left, though all of them, including newly formed Amtrak, still heated their passenger cars with steam, a holdover from days when locomotives like 8444 ruled the rights-of-way. Though the steam locomotive had evolved into a curiosity worthy of exhibition at a world's fair, I realized that the age of steam was not over as long as steam generated by boilers in diesel locomotives pulsed the length of trains to keep passengers warm. During winter months on northern lines, steam lines sometimes leaked in dramatic ways. I loved seeing trains, even diesel-powered ones, enveloped in clouds of steam, and I think this combination resulted in some of my most evocative early images. Some of the pictures had a soft focus reminiscent of the pictorialist school of photography popular in the early twentieth century. Steam was doomed as a way to heat passenger cars, as it had been earlier to haul the trains themselves. Eventually Amtrak and VIA kept their passengers warm by heat from electricity generated aboard the locomotives. With head-end power, the age of steam truly ended.

A Union Pacific freight climbs the steep grade winding up the western slopes of Oregon's Blue Mountains in 1978. Beginning in the 1840s a trail linked Missouri and Oregon, and settlers' wagons struggled to surmount the same range of mountains a short distance from here.

The age of steam was still evident on a bitterly cold day in North Dakota in 1969. Pictured here is the Northern Pacific's *North Coast Limited* heading west to Seattle and Portland.

On a foggy morning in Butte, Montana, in 1969. At the left is the Union Pacific's *Butte Special* running to Salt Lake City, and at the right is the Northern Pacific's *North Coast Limited* running from Seattle to Chicago.

Another of my foggy-morning-in-Butte pictures. The car
on the right brought up the rear of the *Butte Special.*

Sunrise in Whitefish, Montana, in 1972. Steam still heated the cars of Amtrak's *Empire Builder*.

Another of my "pictorialist" images. This one dates from 1969 and shows the steam-wreathed diesel locomotive at the head of the *North Coast Limited* as it pauses in Minneapolis on its way to Chicago.

Burlington Northern freight runs through a basalt landscape along the
north bank of the Columbia River in eastern Washington on tracks of
the former Spokane, Portland, and Seattle Railway in the 1990s.

Portfolio 2

Where Water Meets Rail

Butler Area Public Library
218 North McKean Street
Butler PA 16001

Juxtaposing different modes of transportation in a landscape where water meets rail is visually very appealing to me. Aboard one of the Lindblad boats cruising the Columbia and Snake rivers of the Pacific Northwest, it is hard not to notice different modes of transportation on all sides, though the ostensible purpose of our voyages is to follow, if only in imagination, in the wake of Lewis and Clark, the explorers who paddled these waterways by canoe in 1805 and 1806. Heritage tourism, it is called, and I am convinced that Lindblad Expeditions offers a far richer educational experience than any of its competitors. However, whenever I had any free time I did not try to photograph remnants of the Lewis and Clark expedition, which in any case was not possible apart from the lower hundred miles of the Columbia, because starting in the 1930s the waters impounded by Bonneville and other great dams had drowned all evidence of their campsites and portages. Instead, I aimed my camera lens at towboats and barges or the Union Pacific and Burlington Northern Santa Fe trains that thundered along opposite banks of the Columbia.

In America from the 1830s through the 1860s, railroads and rivers generally had been regarded as complementary forms of transportation. Early railroads often ran in ways that expanded and improved transportation by water. It was mainly after the Civil War that railways and steamboats on the Missouri River and other waterways competed head-to-head, though on the Columbia River the Union Pacific Railroad operated a fleet of steamboats for several decades in addition to its trains. On the upper Missouri, by contrast, where bitter cold temperatures froze the river solid for months, long-distance steamboats never overcame the railroad advantage.

The names of many of America's early railroads refer to the waterways that defined the extent of their aspirations. The Delaware and Hudson, for example, initially sought to link by rail (and canal) those two great river highways of the eastern seaboard. Likewise, the Mohawk and Hudson linked two river corridors across upstate New York. Later, quite a few railroad names addressed their corporate intentions to link the Atlantic or Gulf coasts with the Ohio River: Chesapeake and Ohio; Baltimore and Ohio; and Gulf, Mobile, and Ohio. No body of water, however, compared with the Pacific Ocean as a romantic destination for the railroads of the United States and Canada.

Probably the first railroad to make the word *Pacific* officially part of its corporate title was the Pacific Railroad, which the state of Missouri chartered in the late 1840s. Later, as the Missouri Pacific, it added thousands of miles of track throughout the Midwest and Southwest, but it never surmounted the Rocky Mountains to reach the Pacific Coast. The Chicago, Rock Island, and Pacific likewise extended its tracks west from Lake Michigan to the front range of the Rockies but lacked the financial muscle needed to continue. On the other hand, the Union Pacific; Northern Pacific; Southern Pacific; and even the Chicago, Milwaukee, St. Paul, and Pacific reached the west coast, as did the Canadian Pacific, which in 1885 completed a line stretching from one shore of North America across Canada to the other.

In the years before the war with Mexico and acquisition of California in the late 1840s, the Pacific Ocean in the minds of American expansionists like Senator Thomas Hart Benton of Missouri meant the mouth of the Columbia River. For years he dreamed of some kind of transportation link between his hometown of St. Louis and the lower Columbia River, which he envisioned as the water gateway to the fabulous commercial wealth of China and India. For many people then, the Columbia was the Great River of the West, while today, though tamed by its many dams, it retains a romantic attraction for those who travel aboard the cruise boats that ply its history-laden waters.

Friends often ask why I go back year after year with Lindblad Expeditions to the Columbia River. Apart from the personal pleasure of introducing newcomers to the Great River of the West, my answer is that the landscape is never the same from one trip to another. I have yet to feel the boredom expressed by the phrase "been there, done that." Light filtering through the clouds of a rain storm, for example, might highlight features of the river's scenic passage through the Cascade Mountains that would otherwise be invisible on sunny days. Frankly, I doubt that I will ever capture the Columbia's many subtle and elusive moods with my camera, but therein lies my perennial challenge.

The Joso Trestle has carried Union Pacific trains across the Snake River in eastern Washington since 1914. This one was headed north to Spokane. From there grain-hauling cars often continued north over tracks of the former Spokane International Railroad to pick up loads in western Canada.

Sunrise on the Columbia River near Astoria, Oregon. Railroads did not closely parallel the lower hundred miles of the waterway, but opportunities for maritime photography abounded.

Oceangoing ships cannot travel the Columbia River above Vancouver, Washington. Instead, shallow-draft barges handle all river freight between the Vancouver/Portland area and the ports of Pasco, Washington, and Lewiston, Idaho.

Among Oregon's top scenic attractions is Multnomah Falls. Located on the south bank of the Columbia River as it flows west through a gap in the Cascade Mountains, the falls are easily visible from the waterway. Union Pacific trains once paused here to provide passengers a view of the water as it plunged more than six hundred feet from a mountain ledge to the river below.

Sunrise in Seattle in the early twenty-first century. The large cranes transferred intermodal containers between oceangoing ships and trains.

A northbound Amtrak train passed the *American Orient Express* (right) at the Savannah, Georgia, station.

Portfolio 3

The View from the *American Orient Express*

The *American Orient Express*, should readers not be familiar with that once-glorious train, operated between 1995 and 2008 essentially as a North American rail counterpart to the glamorous cruise ships that Holland America, Cunard, and Carnival use to sail the Seven Seas. In other words, by functioning much as a cruise ship sailing across the United States, Canada, and Mexico, the *American Orient Express* offered many additional possibilities for heritage tourism. A traveler could board the train in Washington, D.C., for example, stow the contents of his or her suitcase in various nooks and crannies of a private room, and spend the next two weeks cruising slowly across America to Los Angeles. The train stopped in Charleston, Savannah, New Orleans, San Antonio, Santa Fe, and at the south rim of the Grand Canyon on its way across the continent to allow guests to tour local sights and enjoy regional cuisine. In northern Mexico the train threaded its way through majestic Copper Canyon, which though not as colorful as Grand Canyon is five times larger! Across Canada between Montreal and Vancouver guests looked forward to crossing the Rocky Mountains and following the serpentine Fraser River Canyon of British Columbia. For me, even the broad prairies of Manitoba, Saskatch-ewan, and Alberta, and the expansive wilderness of the Canadian Shield of Ontario offered photographic opportunities.

The *American Orient Express* included no coaches in its composition. All guests enjoyed private bedrooms and the opportunity to relax in public spaces provided by two lounge cars, an observation car from the New York Central's famed *Twentieth Century Limited*, and two dining cars. A full-time pianist entertained guests in one of the club-like lounge cars. Not even my idealized *Spirit of St. Louis* was that upscale.

My work as an onboard lecturer was light enough to allow plenty of time to photograph the passing landscape from one of the open vestibules. The company also included me in all its off-train tours. I fell in love with the public squares of Savannah, shaded by massive live oaks draped with gossamer Spanish moss. I would gladly have returned to coastal Georgia and South Carolina year after year. Like so many places, the cities of Savannah and Charleston displayed themselves in different ways during each of the four seasons, and even during different hours of the day.

I switched from film to a digital camera in 2002, and that proved a real blessing aboard the *American Orient Express*. With the fold-out screen on my Canon G2 and subsequent cameras I could twist the image this way and that and no longer worry about needing to stick my head out of the train and into a brisk wind to get a forward-looking view. I actually preferred the less-expensive high-end point-and-shoot models to pricy single lens reflexes because after enduring just one year of all types of inclement weather and conditions aboard the *American Orient Express* and the Lindblad cruise boats, my weather-beaten camera had earned an honorable retirement in a display case. It was then time to buy a new one for the next year's adventures.

What I liked most about the *American Orient Express*—in addition to five-star meals on dining-car wheels, the romantic harmonies professional musicians sweet-talked from the train's baby grand piano, and my mobile bedroom—was enjoying the passing landscape from the vestibule of one of its vintage passenger cars. The main purpose of a vestibule was to permit travelers to board or exit cars at station stops and to cross safely between cars while the train was in motion. When the upper part of a vestibule's Dutch door was open, I relished a chance to study the passing scenery from the mobile vantage point.

The invention of the passenger car vestibule in the 1880s was never intended to encourage travelers to interact with the landscape. In fact, just the opposite happened as closed vestibules replaced open platforms once common at the ends of cars. Vestibules were strictly functional, and because they remain so today, they are breezy, noisy, and even dangerous places for passengers to ride when a train is running at high speed. The *American Orient Express* posted notices in all its vestibules that warned: "Do not lean out of open doors or windows!" There was no lawyerly gobbledygook there, but just in case a dimwitted passenger missed the point, the next line added: "Do not place any part of your body outside of the windows!" The next line: "Do not throw any objects from the train!" Finally: "Do not throw ciga-

rettes or other burning material from the train!" In other words, do not interact with the passing landscape in any way except with your eyes, and you should do that only through the windows of passenger cars provided for your sightseeing in air-conditioned comfort.

To me, however, vestibule riding on the *American Orient Express* presented a tantalizing opportunity. Here I could savor the fleeting countryside—and not just its passing sights but also its sounds and smells and feel, to fully absorb America like the poet Walt Whitman had once imagined doing. I wanted to feel the summer's heat and sticky humidity in the piney woods of east Texas or the dryness of the northern Arizona deserts. I wanted to see heat lightning illuminate the Staked Plains surrounding Lubbock, or a setting sun burnish the sands of the Painted Desert near Holbrook, or a gentle breeze tousle the Spanish moss festooning the Cypress trees of a Louisiana swamp. Nature's art inherent in miles of passing landscape could keep me transfixed for hours, and I suppose I have stood at the vestibule window the equivalent of three entire round-trips across the United States, and maybe many more. At times I found it hard to retire to my roomette because I preferred to enjoy the darkened countryside as the train sped through the night.

During daylight hours I enjoyed waving to strangers, especially the children and pretty girls, who were surprised and delighted by the spectacle of a luxury passenger train rolling through a dejected and largely forgotten mill village in rural Georgia or Alabama or Vermont. I always kept a camera in hand to record views of the railroad landscape—the "metropolitan corridor," in the apt words of John Stilgoe—but, of course, no still camera could ever capture the odors and other tactile sensations that made my vestibule vantage point such a pleasure. Vestibule riding aboard the *American Orient Express* provided the luxury of time to reflect

Crossing the Prairie Provinces in July 2003, the *American Orient Express* used tracks
of the Canadian National Railway to travel between Montreal and Vancouver.

on ways travelers across North America historically regarded the passing landscape—and perhaps more importantly, how the vehicle itself, to borrow and adapt a concept made popular by media philosopher Marshall McLuhan, shaped and controlled what people experienced.[6]

In other words: how have different modes of transportation contributed to travelers' perceptions of the landscapes through which they passed, both historically and today? We all know from personal experience how commercial airline passengers in the jet age fail to meaningfully interact with the landscape passing beneath their wings. We leave the airport lounge and board the plane through an enclosed jetway that insulates us from the landscape of the Tarmac. Once in the air, only window seats provide a view of the countryside below, and it is anything but intimate at an altitude of 39,000 feet. Nor, of course, can passengers experience any tactile interaction with the landscape.

To make matters even worse, cabin attendants on long flights ask passengers to lower their window shades so that everyone can view the day's movie in semi-darkness. When we reach our destination, the airport looks rather like the one we left a few hours earlier. Modern air travel distorts spatial reality because passengers have no real sense of the speed they are traveling or of the passing landscape because at high altitudes there are no easily visible reference points. Airlines also consciously seek to amplify the sense of isolation that height creates: it is exceedingly rare, for example, to find a modern airline timetable, brochure cover, or poster that features the ground landscape from the vantage point of a window on a modern jetliner. It is, I might add, exceedingly

rare these days to find a printed timetable for any airline based in the United States.

Modern train travel in North America is almost as isolating. Recently I noticed that a writer aboard Amtrak's *Southwest Chief* describe his "roomette" as having "a plasma screen-sized window" through which to view the landscape. He continued: "That night, I wake up in Kansas to a thunderstorm straight out of *The Wizard of Oz*. Fat bolts of lightning illuminate the wide sky and the plains. It is my own private storm—and I'm happy I'm not on an airplane. The next day is like an eight-hour IMAX travelogue. The flat fields of Kansas give way to the low blond hills and rock-studded mountains of Colorado. By noon we're in New Mexico, passing trading posts, pueblos, and Spanish missions. Late in the afternoon, I sink into a swivel armchair in the observation car for a glass of wine as we travel past awesome red-rock formations." Curiously, in the eyes of this modern travel writer, the train windows and the Southwest scenery became an extension of our television-and-movie-rich popular culture.[7]

Was the landscape beyond his "plasma screen-sized window" real? Or does that sound like a silly question in a world increasingly defined by cyberspace? I have been told, it might be worth noting, that some large cruise ships in Alaska offer closed-circuit broadcasts of the passing landscape, thus allowing passengers to view glaciers and whales on television screens from the comfort of their staterooms. Even if this is an urban myth, it suggests how contemporary travelers find themselves increasingly removed from the landscapes through which they pass. But do they care?

Before American railroads air-conditioned their finest passenger trains in the 1930s, the windows of the cars opened. There was

6. John R. Stilgoe, *Metropolitan Corridor: Railroads and the American Scene*; Marshall McLuhan, *Understanding Media: The Extensions of Man* (New York: McGraw-Hill, 1964).

7. Richard Alleman, "The Rail Deal," *Travel & Leisure* 34 (April 2004): 147.

The *American Orient Express* threaded its way west through Mexico's spectacular Copper Canyon on a sunny day in February 2003. The canyon is supposed to be five-times larger than Arizona's better-known Grand Canyon.

A local passenger train eased past the *American Orient Express* in Mexico's Copper Canyon. On this day in February 2005 the rain fell in torrents, and on the opposite side of the *AOE* I saw a mountain rivulet transformed into a raging river. Fortunately the waters did not rise high enough to reach the tracks.

even a time in the late 1920s and early 1930s before pressurization and streamlining that windows on commercial airplanes opened, too. Travelers in those days could truly interacted with the landscape from the comfort of their seats—or experience a lack of comfort, such as when train passengers sweltered in the noonday heat of the western deserts in mid-summer, or felt smothered by a weighty blanket of humidity rising from a warm Southern swamp, or had their white clothes soiled by grit rising from the right-of-way or soot blown back from the coal- or oil-burning steam locomotive ahead.

A traveler's sense of intimacy with the landscape was even more profound during the age of the overland stagecoach or Missouri River steamboat in the 1850s and 1860s. When the Butterfield Overland Mail inaugurated stagecoach travel between St. Louis and San Francisco in September 1858—providing the first commercial transportation link between the two largest cities of the West—the journey required approximately twenty-five days. That meant plenty of time and opportunity for passengers to interact with the landscape for good or for ill—and much of it seems to have been for ill.

The body of a Concord stagecoach did not have glass windows, only open enclosures covered by leather flaps. Dust kicked up by the hooves of the six spirited horses pulling the coach invariably filtered into the passenger compartment. Because the stage company allowed passengers a maximum of twenty-five pounds of baggage, a weight limit strictly enforced, some travelers took their allotment in whisky, which they treated as a form of anesthesia to numb their senses during the long overland journey. I suspect the landscape meant nothing to them except that the many miles of it added to the tedium of the nearly month-long journey. Alas, travelers by stagecoach in the 1850s had no cameras capable of capturing the passing scene from their moving vehicle, such as I did during my travels aboard the *American Orient Express* between 1995 and 2007.[8]

8. For a nearly complete history of the *American Orient Express* and its successor train, see Karl Zimmermann, *The GrandLuxe Express: Traveling in High Style* (Bloomington: Indiana University Press, 2007). Alas, about a year after Zimmermann's book appeared, the train made its last run in August 2008.

Rails glistened on an overcast day while the American Orient Express paused in Jasper, Alberta. From here guests traveled by motor coach south to view the ever-impressive Columbia Ice Field. Usually I accompanied all the bus excursions, but once in a while a tour leader allowed me to remain behind and spend pleasant hours photographing the local rail landscape and any passing trains.

A fresh rose and a bottle of champagne were among the elegant touches that delighted guests on the *American Orient Express* as they settled into their "compact but cozy" rooms to begin their rail cruise.

The fall colors of New England wreath the *American Orient Express on* one of its trips between Quebec City and Bar Harbor. The train itself went no closer to the Maine coast than a rail yard near Bangor, from which guests continued by motor coach to Bar Harbor. Despite the scenery of Acadia National Park and a feast of fresh lobster in Bar Harbor, this series of trips was not a great success because each one required guests to crawl out of their cozy beds a total of four times during the wee hours of the night to present their passports to border inspectors.

A porter on the *American Orient Express* paused from her work long enough to enjoy the view from the open vestibule as the train sped east from Vancouver and up the Fraser Valley on its lengthy journey across Canada.

Another view from the vestibule: California's Cajon Pass in 2003. Here, trains from the east converge to enter the Los Angeles basin by easing down a steep grade into San Bernardino.

My camera recorded the *American Orient Express* as it traveled east through the Canadian Rockies near the crest of the North American continent.

On tracks that once formed the main line of the Northern Pacific, the *American Orient Express* followed the Yakima River canyon between Yakima and Ellensburg in eastern Washington.

As I stood in the vestibule, one of the challenges that greatly intrigued me was how best to trick a still camera into capturing motion. Here I concentrated on keeping the rails, ballast, and ties sharp while a fast-moving freight blurred past the *American Orient Express* as it waited in a siding.

Using a slow shutter speed, I photographed a tank car as another train bolted past the *American Orient Express*. At times like this, rail photography required a steady camera despite the thunderous noise, irritating track dust, and the rare but life-threatening possibility that debris might fly up from the right-of-way or off the passing train. That was why I preferred a camera with an articulated screen so that I did not have to risk sticking my head into the slipstream to view the action.

This turned out to be my favorite image suggesting speed. Running side by side, the *American Orient Express* and a lengthy coal train thundered east through the Fraser River Valley of British Columbia. Rarely did I see two trains run neck-and-neck in this manner, the only other occasions being on multitrack speedways between San Bernardino and Los Angeles and west from Clovis, New Mexico.

Even when the *American Orient Express* halted for an extended period of time, the view from the vestibule could still be impressive. I recorded the multiple rainbows at Jasper, Alberta, one of my favorite places to photograph the railroad landscape.

The blackness of a fast-approaching thunderstorm highlighted the architectural features that give Bristol's Temple Meads Station the look of a Medieval castle or fortress. The date was 2001, and I had just arrived by express train from London following the line of the former broad-gauge Great Western Railway.

Portfolio 4
Mother of All Railways

Railways such as we would recognize today originated in England's coal regions, primarily the mining country upriver from Newcastle. Before technical geniuses adapted mobile steam engines to power trains in the early nineteenth century, steam had already proved its worth by giving muscle to massive stationary engines used to pump water from mines located deep underground. Some mines used crude wooden or iron rails to make it easier for horses or mules to pull a string of cars loaded with coal or metal ore to river landings.

The most successful early marriage of steam and rail took shape as the Liverpool and Manchester Railway, opened in England in 1830 to transport freight and passengers between its namesake cities, and portent of the coming railway age. No one did more to ensure that the marriage of technologies would be successful than a self-trained engineer named George Stephenson (1781–1848), whose likeness now appears on all Five Pounds currency issued by the Bank of England. Also depicted is his revolutionary 1829 railway locomotive called "Stephenson's Rocket."

American observers, some of whom sailed to England to see for themselves the new technology in action, applied what they learned from the Mother Country to the as-yet-unbuilt railways of the United States. One of the most important was the Baltimore and Ohio, which opened its first miles of track in 1830 and for several years functioned as a university of sorts to teach aspiring civil engineers their trade. At the time not a single college or university in the United States, apart from West Point and a private university in Vermont, offered engineering degrees of any type.

Almost from the beginning, American railroads followed a path that diverged in significant ways from the English. Whereas railroading's Mother Country constructed railways seemingly to last for all time, using brick, stone, and iron to fashion stations and bridges that looked as if they could double as castles and defensive fortifications, cash-poor Americans used wood and took every conceivable construction short-cut, like building wooden stations and trestles and single-track lines with sidings to permit trains to pass one another instead of investing in the double-track main lines favored by the English. American railway lines turned and twisted as they snaked their way through rolling and uplifted terrain to avoid as much as possible the expense of boring tunnels and constructing the massive cuts and fills favored by the English to circumvent steep grades and sharp curves.

On the station platform in Sheffield, England. The brightly painted coaches of Virgin Trains wait in the background. With a Britrail Pass this was an easy day-trip from London aboard one of the Midland Mainline trains.

In addition, England's early railways did what seemed most logical and attached several stagecoach bodies together to form a single passenger car. Even today, some of the older railway cars in Britain still feature individual compartments that open directly onto station platforms. Americans, too, originally used stagecoach bodies on wheeled platforms, but they soon veered off in another direction, building passenger cars that featured long center aisles flanked by bench seats. The new arrangement was more democratic and hence functioned as a statement of American egalitarianism, or so some people have claimed.

Another difference was that though Great Britain and the United States in time adopted the same standard gauge for major railways (4 feet 8 1/2 inches between the rails), British locomotives and cars remained smaller than their American counterparts because it was far too expensive for British railways to re-engineer rights-of-way to accommodate freight and passenger cars and locomotives that grew larger after the American Civil War ended in 1865. The difference can still be seen in British and American trains to this day. Score one for America's fascination with built-in obsolescence that made it easy for the United States to modernize its hastily and cheaply constructed early railways.

England exported its early expertise in railway construction and operation around the world—first to parts of Europe and then to distant India, Australia, South Africa, and even Argentina. The United States played a secondary, but nonetheless significant, role in shaping the evolution of world railways, such as when Russian engineers in the early twentieth century studied the electrification of the Milwaukee Road across the mountains of Montana before adapting it to their country's needs.

England also played a role in giving travel by railways, as opposed to private carriages, some needed social cachet. And therein lies the little-known story of one reluctant train rider named Queen Victoria, who also happened to be the great social arbiter of the early railway age. But first, I must introduce you to Dr. Ruth Chilcott.

Although Dr. Ruth Chilcott had no formal connection to the railways of Great Britain and Europe, she greatly facilitated my appreciation of them. I first met her during an *American Orient Express* cruise across the United States from Washington, D.C., to Los Angeles. I was the onboard lecturer, and Dr. Ruth was a retired psychiatrist from the Bromley area, near London, and one of the train's eighty guests. We became acquainted early in the journey, and thus I had time to amplify for her the rich history and geography of the Sunbelt regions we were crossing.

Dr. Ruth, in turn, regaled me with stories of her life in Britain. After medical school she had married an English husband and raised her family in an upscale suburb of London, though she herself remained proudly Welsh—and God seems to have blessed the Welsh with an ability to dramatize a story by words and body language. Before the *American Orient Express* eased to its final stop in the Los Angeles Union Station, Dr. Ruth had graciously invited me to stop by her home during my first visit to England the following July.

Experience had taught me that a good many guests at the conclusion of a lengthy train or boat journey will invite me to visit them in their homes, but that is merely a fine courtesy. They would be dumbfounded, I am certain, were I to show up on their doorstep in person. However, Dr. Ruth made a point of phoning me twice from England to stress that she wanted my wife and me to stop by her home. We did, and she kindly devoted a full day to giving us an automobile tour of the lovely country landscape of Kent and East Sussex. We could not have asked for a more congenial companion. Her wickedly witty commentaries on England

According to locals, the architect's plans for Melbourne's Flinders' Street Station were supposed to have been shipped from the Mother Country to Bombay, India, but somehow ended up in Australia instead.

and the English from her Welsh perspective were all the more entertaining because this was our first trip to Great Britain.

A short time after I returned to the United States, Ruth Bryant, a retired vice-president of the Federal Reserve Board in St. Louis and chairperson of the St. Louis Mercantile Library Board, invited me to speak to the local English-Speaking Union on the subject of kings and queens riding the trains of Great Britain. I immediately thought of Dr. Ruth Chilcott because I very much needed her help. I knew far more about the mundane details of railway history in Great Britain than I did about the specific subject of royalty and railways.

I confidently expected to find the history I needed at the British Library, where I had a researcher's card, and at the National Railway Museum in York, which is without doubt the finest museum of its type in the world. But for good measure I wrote to Dr. Ruth to see what she might know about the subject. She was a physician and not a rail historian, after all, and so I did not expect much.

A short time later I received a trans-Atlantic phone call, and Dr. Ruth asked me, "Dear Carlos, how would you like to tour the old royal station at Sandringham?" That facility, which is located in the idyllic village of Wolferton and only a short carriage ride from the royal palace and the Queen's Estate of Sandringham, had not been opened to the public for years. In fact, I misspeak here because as a royal station I'm not sure it was ever open to the public.

The last royal train departed there in 1966 and the tracks themselves had been removed in 1969, all in response to Dr. Richard Beeching's infamous report that urged Britain's Conservative government to close lightly used railway lines across the country. The station buildings were almost demolished to provide space to build private homes; fortunately, the historic station buildings survived. One is now a private residence, and the other was refur-

bished and offered for sale in 2001 at an asking price of £750,000. Should Queen Elizabeth choose to travel by train to her Sandringham Estate today, she would find that the nearest railway station was located in Kings Lynn, about nine miles away. Most often the Queen uses a helicopter to journey between her Windsor and Sandringham estates.

The little Wolferton station retains its rich history. Though it has been remodeled and expanded over the decades by the addition of several waiting rooms, original portions of the building date to the early 1860s. Built initially to accommodate royal trains to and from the Sandringham Estate in Norfolk that Queen Victoria's son, the Prince of Wales, purchased in the 1860s, the Wolferton station was a silent witness to the arrival in 1863 of the Prince and his bride, Princess Alexandra, following their marriage at Windsor in 1863. The future King Edward VII spent his honeymoon at Sandringham. Years later when one of the couple's sons, the mentally unbalanced Duke of Clarence, celebrated his twenty-first birthday at Sandringham, a circus elephant rented for the merriment escaped and nearly destroyed the entrance to the Wolferton station.

The little railway station also witnessed the arrival and departure of the future King Edward VII's many mistresses. Likewise, it offered a clandestine retreat for his grandson Edward VIII when he met for a romantic interlude with Wallis Warfield Simpson. Most improbably, the mad Russian monk Rasputin was reputed to have arrived at Wolferton only to be sent packing by an alert stationmaster.

Between 1884 and 1911 it is probable that royal trains arrived and departed from Wolferton on at least 645 occasions. Unfortunately, I have found no tally of royal trains before or after those years, but the station continued to be well used for years. Following the unexpected death of King George VI at Sandringham in

If only the former Wolferton Station near Sandringham Palace could talk, what a tale of royal comings and goings it could tell. By the summer of 2001 the tracks were long gone, but the structure's exterior still preserved the appearance of a country railway station in England.

February 1952, a royal train carried his body from Wolferton Station to London, a final journey of ninety-five miles. From King's Cross Station the king's body traveled to Westminster Abbey, where the sorrowing nation paid its last respects. Likewise, the body of his father, King George V, passed to its terrestrial place of rest through the portals of the royal station at Wolferton in 1936 as a band played Chopin's mournful "Funeral March."

When I visited the station more than sixty years later, the waiting rooms that once accommodated the crowned heads of Europe and their relatives and distinguished guests had recently been meticulously restored by a gifted contractor. Dr. Ruth happened to know the right person to give me an insider's tour. She always did, or so it seemed to me.

She had promised to get me into the now-private royal station if my wife and I met her at an appointed hour at the railway station in nearby Kings Lynn. We did, and Dr. Ruth and the two gentlemen involved in the Wolferton restoration and sale escorted us patiently through its many different rooms. With understandable pride, Max and Nigel pointed to a recent photograph of Prince Charles visiting the station to congratulate them on their restoration work. These two men and their craftsmen had overlooked no details. Even the toilet and its original porcelain plumbing (which oddly featured a royal crest inside the urinal of the men's room) had been restored, as if to welcome any royal males seeking relief. Where rails once ran they had planted low shrubs to simulate the tracks.

When we were through, Dr. Ruth insisted on driving us back to London, a trip that included a stop for Evensong in the magnificent cathedral at Ely. It was dark when we reached London, but she gave us an insider's tour of the city. It turned out that she had spent five years of her retirement taking university-level courses on the history of London. She had obviously mastered her subject well.

During my forty years as a professional historian, I have become fully convinced that both life and history are really about making the proper connections, though a good many of them may be serendipitous. Had I not met Dr. Ruth I am sure my familiarity with things English (and Welsh) would have been limited. She told me, for instance, that when she was a girl growing up in southern Wales, the Great Western Railway that the Victorian engineering genius Isambard Kingdom Brunel extended west from London's Paddington Station to Bristol and Cardiff was known by its initials, GWR—"God's Wonderful Railway." How appropriate to describe a railway pioneer who insisted on building the Great Western to the widest gauge in the world.

It was on "God's Wonderful Railway" that young Queen Victoria took her first train ride. She was Great Britain's first reigning monarch to travel by train. The Queen's historic trip took place on June 13, 1842, and Isambard Kingdom Brunel himself climbed aboard the locomotive to help direct the royal train, which huffed and puffed its way from Slough Station located near Windsor Castle to London's Paddington Station.

The newfangled railway technology worried Queen Victoria's royal coachman, who urged Britain's young monarch not to endanger herself by making the journey, but Prince Albert assured the Queen that he had ridden Brunel's trains many times since 1839 when he had come to court her at Windsor Castle. Victoria always trusted her beloved Prince Albert. Britain's first royal train consisted of six carriages, including a royal salon upholstered in a sprightly combination of white silk and crimson.

The royal coachman must have cursed fate as he climbed aboard the hissing mechanical monster and dutifully stationed himself on the locomotive footplates with Brunel and Daniel Gooch, the Great Western's locomotive superintendent. On several occasions during the short journey, Victoria's nervous coachman

The author and Dr. Ruth Chilcott at her Bromley home outside London in 2002.

insisted on taking the locomotive controls, insisting that it was part of his royal duty. By the time the special train reached London's Paddington Station approximately thirty minutes later, the royal coachman must have thoroughly regretted his impromptu decision to ride the footplates, because thick smoke and red-hot cinders blown back from the locomotives hard-puffing stack had blackened, singed, and thus effectively ruined his scarlet jacket. The poor man refused to ride a train of any type again.

The adventure, on the other hand, delighted the young queen, who insisted that she was "quite charmed" by the railway journey. She continued to travel comfortably and confidently by royal train during the rest of her long reign, her last journey being from a station located near Balmoral Castle in Scotland to Windsor on November 6, 1900. Nonetheless, Victoria insisted that train personnel follow certain protocol of the queen's devising. Foremost, she did not enjoy speed. Following her first train trip from Slough to London, Prince Albert probably spoke for the Queen when he supposedly said, "Not so fast next time, Mr. Conductor." Thereafter Victoria's special train was limited to a top speed of forty miles per hour during daylight hours or thirty miles per hour at night. Likewise, the queen refused to eat meals as long as the royal train was in motion, or to cross between its sitting and sleeping coaches until the train was fully stopped. It would not resume its journey until attendants had properly tucked the Queen into bed. Victoria, by the way, never used modern amenities like electric lights aboard her royal train even after they became widely available.

Although two railway stations served Windsor Castle, Queen Victoria invariably preferred to travel by way of Brunel's Great Western Railway that ran through Slough on its way to Paddington Station. Perhaps that was because she trusted Brunel, or because Paddington Station featured a private royal entrance and a royal waiting room hung with bright silver and pink silk. Even in the early twenty-first century, royalty bound for Windsor Castle still used platform one of Paddington Station.

The fact that Queen Victoria rode that first train in 1842 seemed to place the stamp of royal approval on the relatively new technology, and this, in turn, contributed to additional enthusiasm for railway construction projects in Great Britain. So great was the eagerness of investors to finance railroad projects, some of which were of dubious merit, that the time is known in

British history as "the railway mania." Before the bubble burst in the late 1840s with devastating financial results, construction of engineering projects of all types—tunnels, bridges, stations—went forward with remarkable speed. Many of the structures remain marvels of technology and aesthetics to this day.

When Queen Victoria first rode the rails in 1842, not even two decades had passed since the world's first passenger-carrying railroad opened for business between Stockton and Darlington, England, in 1825. Five years later the formal opening of the Liverpool and Manchester Railway was a public occasion that attracted fifty thousand onlookers. Among the honored guests were the Duke of Wellington, Sir. Robert Peel, and a pro-railway member of Parliament, William Huskisson. Alas, poor Huskisson suffered a fatal accident that day, and his death temporarily heightened popular fears of railway travel. In both Britain and America, railway accidents were common enough to give Victoria's royal coachman legitimate cause to worry. Thus in the 1840s it still took some daring for anyone to climb aboard a train. Queen Victoria deserves credit for her courage in 1842.

As important as Queen Victoria's first railway journey was, the world's first dedicated royal coach was built by the London and Birmingham Railway in 1842, the same year as Queen Victoria's first ride. British railway passenger accommodations at the time all featured stagecoach-like bodies joined together to form a single car. The first occupant of the royal coach was Queen Adelaide, widow of King William IV and aunt to Queen Victoria, who used it on several occasions to visit friends in the British Midlands. The royal coach so impressed Queen Adelaide's German cousin, King Ernest Augustus of Hanover, that he ordered an exact duplicate built for himself to use in the German states.

Curiously, while a good many royal railway cars ended up being scrapped when more modern equipment became available, the royal coach first used by Queen Adelaide somehow survived. In fact, it is on public display in the National Railway Museum in York. Well before that, the world's first royal railway coach traveled all the way to St. Louis in 1904, where it was on display as part of Great Britain's contribution to the city's World's Fair that year.

Looking to the future, I suspect that if I chose to write something about kings and queens of Britain taking to the air, I dare not mention it to Ruth Chilcott. She might take up the challenge to get me aboard a royal airliner or something equally improbable. I once casually mentioned to her that my oldest son was a history major at the University of Pittsburgh, and so during the course of our motor trip through Kent and East Sussex where should we end up? The ancestral estate of William Pitt, the Earl of Chatham. For the life of me I cannot remember whether it was Pitt the elder or Pitt the younger.

A resolute Queen Victoria stands forever on guard outside Belfast City Hall in Northern Ireland.

The Westminster Station of London's Underground (or "Tube")
is located in the historic heart of the mother of all railways.

London's Underground gave the world the phrase "Mind the Gap," a reference to the dangerous open space between the platform and the subway cars.

In the summer of 2001, London's St. Pancras Station was a glorious if some-what shabby architectural confection. Eurostar trains inaugurated high-speed service between refurbished St. Pancras Station and Paris in November 2007.

From under the cavernous train shed of London's Paddington Station, the trains of "God's Wonderful Railway" ran west to Wales and other distant parts of the United Kingdom.

The busy interior of Central Station in Glasgow, Scotland.

The Chateau Frontenac in Quebec City was one of the magnificent hotels built by the Canadian Pacific Railway. After its tracks joined one coast of Canada with the other in 1885, the Canadian Pacific viewed itself as helping extend the imperial reach of the Mother Country around the world to Australia via an "All-Red Route," a reference to the usual color of the British Empire lands as depicted on contemporary maps of the world. Rule Britannia!

The Canadian National Railway, a much younger sibling of the Canadian Pacific, dated from the end of World War I and the Dominion's creation of one nationalized carrier that combined several of the country's insolvent railways. Like the investor-owned Canadian Pacific, the Canadian National ran from coast to coast and helped bind together far-flung nations that comprised the British Empire and later the Commonwealth. In 1976 the railroad completed the world's tallest free-standing structure, the CN Tower in Toronto.

Jasper, Alberta, where Canadian National trains heading west
began their steep ascent to the crest of the Rocky Mountains.

Eurostar trains provided high-speed service between Paris and London by way of a 31.4 mile-long tunnel bored under the English Channel. Travelers saw nothing inside the dark tunnel, but during the ride it was worth contemplating the feat of engineering that made the trans-national connection possible.

Portfolio 5

The Train Gods Must Be Crazy

Aboard a Eurostar Italia train from Venice to Florence I first heard about the "train god." At first the term failed to register on me because I was too busy settling into my reserved seat aboard one of Italy's finest high-speed trains. Fortunately, the recorded "welcome aboard" announcement was broadcast several more times, first in Italian and then in English. Finally I understood, and a thought popped mischievously into mind: yes, of course, "The Train Gods Must be Crazy," an oblique reference to a popular movie. It turned out that the Italian recording in English really referred to the conductor, or the "train guard," but when spoken in the King's English the words came out as "train god." This was not my introduction to the subtle pleasures of riding the trains of Europe, but it remains one of the more memorable moments.

My first trip to the Continent took place in 2002 aboard one of the speedy Eurostar trains linking London and Paris (and a carrier unrelated to Eurostar Italia). The train ambled along conventional tracks in England but then picked up speed noticeably in the 30–mile-long bore under the English Channel, bursting forth like a cannonball on the French side to attain its full stride of 300 kilometers per hour (186 miles per hour). One result is that residents of southern England lived closer to Paris in terms of time

than to London, though the spatial anomaly disappeared after the British opened their new high-speed line into the heart of London in 2007.

The United States once was a world leader in high-speed trains, but the Japanese moved to the fore when they introduced the "Bullet Train" in 1964. The world of high-speed ground travel has never been the same. The French made it a matter of national policy to construct a network of high-speed rail lines radiating out from Paris. The fastest of these *TGV* (*Train à Grande Vitesse*) lines operate over tracks engineered for high-speed trains only, though the high-speed trains are capable of operating over conventional track as well. Germany, likewise, has its *ICE* (InterCity Express) high-speed trains, and Spain has its *Aves* sprinting between Madrid, Seville, and Barcelona. European countries continue to extend the network of high-speed lines so that one day it will be possible to zip from London to Lisbon aboard high-speed trains.

During May 2008 I spent a couple of hours on the platform of the Wilmington, Delaware, Amtrak station on one of the busiest stretches of passenger railroad in the United States. The station, formerly belonging to the Pennsylvania Railroad, is located above city streets and thus sunlight bathes its open platforms to facilitate photography, in marked contrast to the stygian depths of Amtrak platforms in Baltimore, Philadelphia, and New York. Amtrak's highest speed trains, all named *Acela*, zip between Boston, New York, and Washington along the electrified Northeast Corridor, but their top speed is only 150 miles-per-hour, almost leisurely by current Japanese and European standards. In terms of interior design and comfort, though, the *Acela*s rank with the best trains of Europe. However, in contrast to the airplane-style aisles and seats of American trains (the so-called "democratic style"), some of the European high-speed trains employ glass partitions to preserve the tradition of individual compartments.

Of all the nations of Europe, Switzerland probably has the most impressive and interesting railroad network. Famed for their frequency and punctuality, Switzerland's network of trains (and postal buses) intermeshes as seamlessly as the polished gears of an expensive Swiss watch. Because their land is so mountainous, the Swiss excel at feats of railroad engineering, boring long tunnels and erecting spectacular bridges that make any journey a feast for the eyes. On a continent having a history of widespread government ownership of railroads, Switzerland nonetheless has many private lines coexisting with the Swiss Federal Railways.

It is interesting to watch as Swiss railroad conductors switch seamlessly from making announcements in French to German or Italian as trains cross from one language area of the country to another. The lines of demarcation are invisible to an outsider but are clear to the "train god," who knows where announcements for station stops begin with "Meine Damen und Herren" instead of "Mesdames et Messieurs." In other nations the change of language occurs at a national border, and it is part of the process of switching locomotives and train crews. Border guards on trains passing to or from the new eastern members of the European Union still make a ritual out of stamping passports. Crossing the border

between Bulgaria from Romania on a hot summer day with all car windows open for maximum ventilation (and relief from the many cigarette smokers), I heard loud screams coming from the cars ahead. Soon I learned the reason why. Railroad workers ran the entire train through a powerful car wash without warning passengers to shut their windows, and thus gave travelers as well as car windows a thorough dousing. Welcome to Romania!

Passenger trains crossing from France to Spain have adjustable axles on their bogies (or trucks) that can be expanded or contracted to change between the standard gauge width that prevails in France and most of the continent and broad-gauge tracks of Spain and Portugal. Gauge variations do not make any difference in terms of passenger comfort, but they would make it difficult for the trains of an invading army to speed across the border—or so goes one of the explanations as to why Spain, Portugal, and Russia (and other nations of the former Soviet Union) have broader gauges than the rest of Europe. Likewise, Canadian railroads in the middle nineteenth century used a broader gauge than was common in much of the United States, but less for reason of national defense than because of the intense localism that prevailed among North American railroads until the 1880s, when a standard-gauge North American rail network finally took shape.

One of the most dramatic of border crossings occurs on trains linking Hamburg, Germany, with Copenhagen, Denmark. The self-powered cars run aboard a large ferry boat for a journey of more than an hour across an arm of the Baltic Sea. For the duration, train passengers can go up to the open decks and enjoy the fresh salt air. In the United States, passenger trains once ferried across the Hudson River, San Francisco Bay, the lower Mississippi River, and the Columbia River to reach their destinations, but no more. Either bridges or tunnels have been constructed or the

A uniformed guard collected tickets on a train across Eastern Europe in July 2007. However, not all conductors in Bulgaria wore uniforms, which to me was disconcerting because I did not wish to give my ticket to a stranger who looked no different from the passengers. Clean and neatly pressed uniforms, whether worn by commercial airline pilots or railroad passenger conductors, send a message of reassurance to passengers. American railroads enforced a stringent dress code among their uniformed employees.

trains discontinued. In Europe another train ferry operates also across the Strait of Messina separating the toe of the Italian boot from Sicily.

Making Europe such a pleasure is the availability of passes for sale in the United States that offer nearly unlimited train travel—though reservations are still required on the best trains. Travelers can come and go more or less as they please and see what pure serendipity brings them. Making a trip from Dublin to Limerick I mistakenly boarded a crowded second-class train earlier than the first-class one I intended to take. One of the few seats available was next to an older gentleman who turned out to have written several books on the history of Irish church architecture and to my mind was thus the ideal travel companion as we crossed the emerald-green landscape. Patrick Conlan was not wearing his priestly garb, but it did not take me long to learn his vocation. And yet apart from the mysterious workings of pure serendipity I would have missed this opportunity. Father Conlan, on the other hand, would probably have suggested that a Being supremely more powerful than the "train gods" determined a passenger's fate. Based on my numerous positive experiences riding the trains of Europe, I would agree with him.

The train that went to sea. Passengers traveling between Copenhagen and Hamburg in the early twenty-first century enjoyed a relaxing break aboard the ferry that transported their Danish-made coaches across an arm of the Baltic Sea too wide to bridge. The train itself was parked deep inside the ferry.

From Dublin to Limerick in 2008, my ever-informative seat companion was Father Pat Conlan.

A smiling attendant aboard the Russian train just about to depart Helsinki, Finland, for the international run to St. Petersburg, in June 2006.

Passengers aboard a Spanish train linking Madrid and Barcelona in late 2003. The traveler on the right is my son, Matt, now an electrical engineer. The handsome but seemingly sad-faced traveler on the left made me think of the El Greco portraits I had recently seen in Madrid's famous Prado museum.

A German train crossed the Rhine River as it departed Cologne.

InterCity 436

Norddeich Mole–Recklinghausen–

Oberhausen–Düsseldorf Flughafen ✈–

Düsseldorf–Köln–Bonn–Koblenz–Trier–

Luxembourg

DB AG/GB Fernverkehr/NL Köln Umi F4560 (9/24) Fpl 2005

With signs like these posted in the vestibule, it was hard to become lost when traveling aboard a German intercity train.

It was the end of the Christmas holiday season and these bone-weary travelers were on their way from Sicily to Rome aboard a much overbooked train. Angry passengers had nearly rioted because Trenitalia's computer glitch denied them the seats they had reserved. A show of force by police during the stop at Villa San Giovanni helped to keep the peace. As a bilingual Sicilian passenger aptly phrased it to me, "Italy is an unpredictable mix of exhilaration and exasperation."

Even a "train god" cannot interrupt a young traveler's cell phone call.

A fleet of taxis awaited passengers outside New York's Grand Central Terminal on a rainy April day in 2007.

Portfolio 6

Cathedrals of Commerce

Thinking of "train gods," the ancient Romans had one (of sorts). His name was Terminus, god of boundary markers and eventually of end points. Thus railroad stations in the largest cities have come to be called terminals.

A metropolitan terminal was always a special place. In the largest cities and on major railroads, it declared through architecture the importance of the metropolis and the impressive power of the railroad company that built the station. Grand Central Terminal in New York bespoke the power of the New York Central Railroad and its no-nonsense founder, Cornelius Vanderbilt, the self-styled "Commodore" whose steamboats and railroads made him one of the richest men in America. When the *Twentieth-Century Limited* was the Central's premier train between New York and Chicago, attendants ceremoniously rolled out a real red carpet for guests boarding the cars in Grand Central Terminal. Not to be outdone, the Central's great rival bored through the muck under the Hudson River and leveled blocks of New York real estate to erect the magnificent Pennsylvania Station and inaugurate passenger service to the heart of Gotham in 1910.

These two great stations and others like them have been likened to cathedrals of commerce. Just as the Middle Ages witnessed the rise of magnificent cathedrals that testified to a people's faith and the overarching power of the Catholic Church, the late nineteenth and early twentieth centuries witnessed the construction of numerous imposing railroad stations from Melbourne to Montreal that testify to the power of railroads to redefine spatial relationships, extend the reach of European empires, dominate land commerce, and generate huge personal fortunes for canny investors.

A generation of railroad empire builders erected monuments to themselves in these stone-and-steel cathedrals of commerce, just as popes and other religious potentates had done earlier. Besides, corporate modesty was no virtue during the railway age, a time of strident boosterism throughout the American West. When James J. Hill, the no-nonsense boss of the Great Northern Railway, seemed content with an unassuming wooden station to serve Seattle, his West Coast terminus after 1893, proud urban boosters pressured him to build a monumental structure celebratory of their city's emergence as a metropolis of the Pacific Rim. Eventually, the tight-fisted Hill relented and the Great Northern Railway opened Seattle's opulent King Street Station in 1906. It featured a tall Venetian campanile worthy of an honored place on St. Mark's Square itself.

Architecturally imposing railway terminals are a feature of almost every great European city today, with the newest one being the glass-and-steel edifice opened in 2007 to serve Berlin, capital of reunited Germany. London has several terminal stations in the traditional architecture of the high Victorian era, though one of the grandest, St. Pancras (located next to the British Library), was resurrected from its state of dowdy decay and returned to its former glory to serve Eurostar trains linking London and Paris.

North America's railway empire builders and some of their heirs left an architectural legacy the included not only some of the world's most imposing railway terminals, but also hotels and private homes that underscored economist Thorstein Veblen's description of the "conspicuous consumption" that defined the Gilded Age at end of the nineteenth century. James J. Hill had a mansion on Summit Avenue in St. Paul, Minnesota, that is now a museum. Two Vanderbilt brothers used their New York Central millions to build themselves sumptuous summer palaces in Newport Rhode, Island, and another Vanderbilt heir erected the largest private home in the United States on his vast Biltmore estate outside Asheville, North Carolina. Henry Villard of the Northern Pacific built a magnificent home in the heart of New York City that is now an upscale hotel. Henry Huntington's railroad fortune provided the foundation for the fabulous Huntington Museum and Gardens near Pasadena, California.

Finally, there is Henry Flagler, in a class of his own. As a partner with John D. Rockefeller in the Standard Oil Trust, he made his first fortune. Hoping to improve the health of his first wife, he grew interested in Florida and its climate, using his oil millions to buy a small railroad and extend it all the way from Jacksonville to Key West, by way of Miami, one of numerous settlements along with Palm Beach that his Florida East Coast Railroad fa-

thered. He built many grand hotels in Florida, with the grandest being The Breakers in Palm Beach. With this magnificent resort and its surrounding upscale community, Flagler could play his own game of "one-upmanship" with the old-money blue bloods who dominated the social scene at the long-established resorts of Saratoga Springs, New York, and Newport, Rhode Island. As a summer home for his third wife, Flagler built Whitehall, which today is a Palm Beach museum showcasing the opulence of the Gilded Age.[9]

The Florida East Coast, the Southern Pacific, and the Santa Fe were three of a handful of railroads in the United States that built luxury resort hotels. The story was much different in Canada. There the Canadian Pacific and the later Canadian National built a series of grand hotels along their tracks that stretched from sea to sea (much as some railroads of Europe had done). One of the grandest of these Canadian railroad hotels is the Empress in Victoria, British Columbia; another is the Chateau Frontenac in Quebec City, the site of one of the major conferences of World War II. It was an edifice fit for the world's kings, queens, prime ministers, and presidents, not to mention ordinary business barons.

Many of the grand railroad hotels still stand, as do the mansions of the railroad potentates and their heirs. The United States and Canada still have magnificent railway terminals serving Amtrak or VIA passengers in Washington, Philadelphia, Chicago, Kansas City, Seattle, Los Angeles, Toronto, Winnipeg, and Vancouver, as well as in several lesser cities, but the two nations have

9. Gregg M. Turner, *A Journey into Florida Railroad History* (Gainesville: University Press of Florida, 2008).

Outside another of America's cathedrals of commerce: Philadelphia's 30th Street Station in June 2008. Riding from here to Wilmington, Delaware, aboard one of the commuter trains operated by the Southeastern Pennsylvania Transportation Authority (SEPTA), I had a conductor demand that I erase all pictures I had taken aboard his train, and he stood by to make certain that I did. He was only doing his job, I suppose, but when I got home to St. Louis one of the first things I did was to purchase a camera that featured *two* separate media slots and the ability to switch quickly between them. On what is now my decoy card I created an innocuous set of images for future use in sticky situations like the one that caught me by surprise in Pennsylvania. It may seem perverse, but for me the more challenging the hunt, the greater the thrill of photographic successes.

The Seaboard Airline Railway built an attractive station in West Palm Beach when it extended tracks south from central Florida in the mid-1920s to serve the young and rapidly growing metropolis of Miami. Amtrak and the commuter trains to Ft. Lauderdale and Miami use the station today.

also witnessed the thoughtless demolition of station structures, both large and small. New York's architecturally imposing Pennsylvania Station New York was torn down so that Madison Square Garden, a mundane structure, could be built atop the waiting area and train platforms. A few blocks across Manhattan, Grand Central Terminal survives in better shape, though the king of stations now wears a mismatched crown formed by the one-time Pan-Am building. The little town of Moscow, Idaho, where I taught history for nearly two decades, once could boast of three separate railroad stations, but today all three are gone. Two of Spokane's three great railroad stations disappeared along with several other downtown structures to make way for its 1974 fair. Only the old Northern Pacific station survives to serve Amtrak and Greyhound passengers. Who can explain the rhyme or reason of survival or demolition?

Fortunately, many architecturally arresting stations escaped the wrecker's ball, though not changes in the railroad landscape. The St. Louis Union Station is still a magnificent facility both inside and out, but no regularly scheduled trains stop there. It functions strictly as a hotel and shopping complex. Cincinnati's art deco Union Station houses the local historical society as well as serving the city's Amtrak passengers, while Union Station in Indianapolis briefly enjoyed rebirth as a hotel and shopping complex on the St. Louis model, though the mall closed in 1997. The building now houses several different organizations, including the local Mexican Consulate and the Indiana Museum of African American History.

It is in Europe that the great railroad stations have maintained their architectural grandeur and long-standing prominence in civic life. Rarely is a major terminal located on an obscure side street or reduced to a prefabricated structure under a highway viaduct, as was true for the Amtrak station in St. Louis (often derided as the "Amshack") until a new intermodal station open late in 2008. Most European rail stations, at least in the continent's western and central nations, form centerpieces for all types of coordinated municipal transportation. Tram lines in cities as widely separated as Berlin, Vienna, and Amsterdam fan out from the railway terminals to serve distant parts of the metropolis, as do suburban commuter lines and often subways, and electric trolley bus and diesel-powered bus lines.

During the twentieth century, the American love affair with the automobile has resulted in such great spatial diffusion (call it "sprawl") in the cities of the United States and Canada that it is difficult to imagine how a centralized station in North America could function as efficiently as one in a relatively more compact European city. It is not surprising that more and more corporations are locating subsidiaries in Europe because of the highly integrated system of public transportation that radiates from its cathedrals of commerce.

A sand-sculpting contest in August 2007 added an artistic touch
to Berlin's Hauptbahnhof, the newest big-city station in Europe.

The dramatic interior of Berlin's multilevel Hauptbahnhof.

Advertising art intended to catch the attention of travelers at the train station in Bari, Italy. I was never bored traveling the trains of Italy, if only because I needed to remain on guard against the ubiquitous pick-pockets. Among my 2008 photos not included in the present portfolios was one of a youthful pickpocket led away in handcuffs by police, who have recently increased their presence in trains and stations in Italy.

Inside the cathedral of commerce serving Bergen, Norway. It was June, but trains traveling between here and the national capital of Oslo would pass through an area of high-mountain snow.

A winter sunrise in Lucerne, Switzerland. Even after the city gained
a modern railway station, the façade of the old one was preserved.

Exterior details from the main train station in Zagreb, Croatia, in 2005.

Is it a cathedral or the cavernous waiting room of Chicago's Union Station? All Amtrak trains serving the Windy City and several of Chicago's commuter rail lines currently use this station.

For comparison's sake: the interior of St. Peter's Basilica in Rome.

My vote for the world's most beautiful location to start or conclude a railway journey goes to Venice's Santa Lucia Station on the city's Grand Canal.

An object worthy of contemplation is the World War II memorial in Luxembourg's main station—but do busy travelers even notice the monument?

Orderly travelers march to their trains through one of Germany's spacious railway stations.

The Union Station in St. Louis, Missouri, still makes a dramatic architectural statement, though it no longer serves the city's train travelers.

Details from the interior of the St. Louis Union Station.

Skyline and rails: the Cologne station as juxtaposed with one of Germany's most famous landmarks, the Kölner Dom, which is the largest Gothic cathedral in northern Europe.

Smoke may be out of fashion today, but to me it still looks glorious when billowing back from a fast-running steam locomotive, like the one Union Pacific still operates for special occasions. This picture comes from southern Idaho.

Portfolio 7

Smokestacks, Skyscrapers, and the Railroad Landscape

As a boy I was always fascinated by smoke—the thicker and blacker the plume rising from a row of smokestacks, the better. For me the highlight of any trip on the Pennsy between Washington and Indianapolis was seeing the glow of the trackside steel mills of Johnstown and Pittsburgh, Pennsylvania, their crimson flames illuminating great plumes of smoke against the nighttime sky. Here was irrefutable evidence of American muscle. In my grade-school geography class in the mid 1950s I learned (along with most other Indiana school children) that the United States was the world's leading producer of oil, copper, steel, and most other basic commodities needed by industry. As I recall it now, as a nation we were deficient only in tin. The smoke of heavy industry along the Pennsylvania tracks confirmed what I learned in school.

I never aspired to own a factory and no one in my family smoked tobacco, but I greatly enjoyed burning leaves in the fall, as well as our family's weekly trash. Back in the prosperous 1950s I never considered a relationship between smoke and environmental degradation. I do not believe, in fact, that most Americans did back then. As I recall it, factory smoke in those days clearly symbolized power and prosperity.

During the first half of the 1950s, when as a boy I lived along-side the main line of the Pennsylvania Railroad east of Indianapolis, I watched steam locomotives pass our back door, huffing and puffing as they hauled long strings of freight cars across central Indiana. By contrast, I thought diesel locomotives pulling the Pennsy's fast passenger trains were uninspiring. I much preferred impressive displays of smoke and steam, the massive drive wheels, and the deep-throated whistles of steam locomotives.

An observer standing beside the tracks could see a steam locomotive coming from miles away as a telltale plume of smoke in the distance darkened the heartland sky. The new diesel locomotives were flashy, but they tended to sneak up on a person, and they left little sign of their passing. But when a steam engine roared by, the acrid-sweet smell of coal smoke might linger in the air for several minutes.

Given our language's many everyday expressions involving smoke, it would seem that I am not the only person intrigued by the subject. For instance, we communicate by sending "smoke signals," or we deceive and obfuscate by "blowing smoke." We mislead with "smoke and mirrors"; we make dubious political choices in "smoke-filled rooms"; and we hide something important behind a "smokescreen" of meaningless words. In an earlier

Smoke from this brightly painted Ferromex diesel seemed almost to qualify it as an "honorary steam engine." The tracks are those of the former Southern Pacific of Mexico.

age, men often relaxed in after-dinner hideaways in which the preferred attire was a "smoking jacket." All-male get-togethers were often called "smokers."

Several years ago I wrote a book about a large copper company based in Arizona. During the many interviews I conducted with employees I heard numerous smoke stories. In one Arizona copper town, a woman of Mexican ancestry told me that as a girl she had dared complain to her father about the smelter smoke that often hung thick in the air. A smelter worker himself, the father marched his daughter outside, pointed skyward to the smokestack, and reminded her, "No smoke, no beans." In industrial America, a smoking stack symbolized factories at work and fat paychecks.

Another thing I learned from my copper town interviews was that some smelter workers believed that smoke cured colds and influenza. At the first sign of a cold or flu they would head for the fiery and smoke-filled interior of the smelter to breathe deeply of its sulphury fumes. Many old-time copper workers still swear by the curative power of this unorthodox cold remedy. Here, I cannot help but recall the Vicks vaporizer my mother used when my brother and I had colds. We called it the "croup kettle," and it operated on much the same principle of breathing deeply of smelter smoke.

I further learned of the "smoke farming" that took place in some smelter towns. At first I thought that interviewees were teasing me, but they were serious. The copper companies of Arizona, and perhaps of other mining areas as well, operated greenhouses in which they exposed samples of locally grown crops to carefully measured drafts of smelter smoke. The resulting calculations formed the basis for how much a company compensated local farmers if smelter smoke stunted their corn, beans, and other crops. Some company scientists told me in all seriousness that certain flowers, such as marigolds, actually bloomed much better when exposed to smelter smoke. It had something to do with sulphur in the air.

Tall stacks belching thick smoke were once the pride of Pittsburgh, icons of the city's economic prowess. Those of us passing through the Steel City by train could admire what the mills signified, though our journeys took us back into the fresh air of rural Pennsylvania, Ohio, and Indiana. We did not have to live with the less-desirable consequences of Pittsburgh's smoke. The late Fred Rogers of Public Television's "Mr. Roger's Neighborhood" once recalled riding around the Pittsburgh area in a car with his father and even as a youngster being made keenly aware of the close relationship between the smoke of heavy industry and the community's economic well-being. At times it seems that the more smoke, the better, though to Pittsburgh residents the thick smoke often brought darkness at noon. Business executives who worked in the city told me that they always brought an extra white shirt to work because the collar of the first one was soiled black by noon.

How ironic that today not a single steel mill operates in the city that is home to professional football's Pittsburgh Steelers. The city's largest employer currently is the University of Pittsburgh Medical Center. One cannot imagine the brawny Steelers renaming themselves the Pittsburgh Meds. Ironically, too, the tall stacks of United States Steel's former Homestead Works in Pittsburgh are now preserved as decorative sentinels lining a parking lot for a small theater complex and shopping mall. Those smokestacks are all that remains of Andrew Carnegie's vast steel mill complex that was the site of the infamous Homestead strike and violence in 1892. If there is a better representation of America's transition from producer to consumer economies than this odd juxtaposition of iconic but useless smokestacks with a shopping mall, I have yet to find it.

The skyline of Pittsburgh in October 2000. Here the Allegheny and Monongahela Rivers unite to form the Ohio River, the iconic Midwestern waterway that in turn will added its flow to the Mississippi near Cairo, Illinois.

Though the smoke of industry signified the robust economy that made it possible for countless thousands of Pittsburgh residents to shop at Kaufmann's Department Store, the city-leading merchandise emporium, it did not agree with members of the Kaufmann family. What they wanted was a rural weekend retreat easily accessible from Baltimore and Ohio tracks that linked Pittsburgh and Washington. To build their mansion in the Pennsylvania woods they hired architect Frank Lloyd Wright. What Wright gave the Kaufmanns as his antidote to Pittsburgh smoke was "Fallingwater," one of the world's greatest architectural wonders after it was completed in 1937.

Why was it, I have often wondered, that our ancestors in the late nineteenth century tolerated smoke as an integral feature of what might be termed "the Victorian skyline"? Some of them not just tolerated it, but they positively reveled in it. Smoking chimneys were good advertising for any ambitious industrial city, and smoke was featured in many turn-of-the-century promotional brochures. Three decades into the twentieth century, Booth Tarkington, the Indiana author who wrote a Pulitzer–prize winning novel he called the *Magnificent Ambersons*, wrote another book about Indianapolis that focused on the symbolism of the city's smoke. He called the book *Growth*, appropriately enough, and Doubleday published it in 1927. It opens with these words: "There is a midland city in the heart of fair, open country, a dirty and wonderful city nesting dingily in the fog of its own smoke."

As Tarkington understood, smoke was once an integral feature of the skyline of any ambitious city. Skylines, in fact, are another subject I enjoyed photographing both on and off the trains because tracks go to the heart of the metropolis, and there the skyline formed an integral part of a railroad landscape. On occasion while doing research at the New York Public Library I took time to walk to the South Street Seaport complex on the East River in lower Manhattan. From there I could see the Brooklyn Bridge a short distance away. It was sobering to think that for several years after the bridge was completed in 1883 those great masonry towers were the tallest structures in New York.

Curiously, when Gustave Eiffel gave the city of Paris a soaring addition to its skyline back in 1889, critics were not uniformly impressed. One grumbled that the world's tallest man-made structure at the time was "dizzily ridiculous," while another grumble that it resembled a "gigantic factory chimney" thrust into the sky.[10] Chimneys, along with the spires of churches and cathedrals, were the skyscrapers that defined the Victorian skyline. St. Paul's Cathedral remains a prominent feature of London's low-rise skyline, and in New York, the tallest structure antedating the towers of the Brooklyn Bridge was the steeple of Trinity Church at the west end of Wall Street.

In once-smoky Pittsburgh, the air is clear these days, and depending on the sunlight, the skyline fairly glistens. Among the prominent structures defining the city's skyline is the PPG Building, a skyscraper designed by Phillip Johnson. It is essentially a model in glass of the famous towers of Parliament in London. Few if any cities can boast of a more dramatic highway entrance than Pittsburgh, especially at night when a motorist emerges from the east portal of the Fort Pitt tunnel into a dazzling panorama as light from tall buildings is reflected by the three rivers that define the city.

That said, with the exception of the PPG Building, I do not think Pittsburgh can claim a signature skyline. That is the kind of

10. David P. Billington, *The Tower and the Bridge: The New Art of Structural Engineering* (Princeton: Princeton University Press, 1985 reprint of 1983 edition): 61.

From the windows of trains across Eastern Europe in 2007 it was common to see abandoned factories and derelict smoke-stacks, a visible consequence of the collapse of Communism and its inefficiencies of production. At times it seemed that all the smoke was aboard the trains, as witnessed in this photograph taken as a Turkish train paused for a station stop in Bulgaria.

skyline so instantly recognizable that it becomes a city's distinctive physical signature. Few places in the world can claim such skylines. For those that do (and this is usually the result of one or two structures that have achieved iconic status), the city skyline becomes a marketable commodity both for tourists as well as for consumers of its best-known products. In the United States I believe that San Francisco, Seattle, St. Louis, Chicago, Washington, and New York can claim to have signature skylines because of the Trans-America Pyramid and the Golden Gate Bridge, the Space Needle, the Gateway Arch, the Sears Tower, the Washington Monument, and the Empire State Building (and until September 11, 2001, the twin towers of the World Trade Center), respectively. I do not think the same could be claimed for Norfolk, Indianapolis, or Phoenix, for example. Cleveland's Terminal Tower, though built in the early 1930s, still dominates the city's skyline. Once it was the tallest structure between New York and Chicago.

Some of my favorite illustrations from the past portrayed railroad landscapes against a backdrop of tall structures that defined a generic skyline, the tracks stretching horizontally, the buildings reaching vertically, and for good measure smoke from steam locomotives in the foreground wreathing the whole scene. That was when brawny Pittsburgh was an appropriate metaphor for America. The juxtaposition of trains, tall buildings, and even the surrounding smoke affirm that America was confident of its place in the world and its rock-solid prosperity. No wonder I get nostalgic for that brawny United States when I hear "Smoke Gets in Your Eyes," a hit tune from 1933: "When a lovely flame dies, smoke gets in your eyes."

The cover image from a 1949 brochure combined trains, monuments, and skyscrapers to advertise the Pennsy's new *Liberty Limited*, a streamliner linking Chicago and Washington by way of Pittsburgh.

The *American Orient Express* arrived in Montreal, Quebec, at the end of a long rail cruise that began on the opposite side of Canada in Vancouver.

The skyline of another Canadian metropolis, Toronto, as viewed at twilight from the vestibule of the *American Orient Express*. At the center of the picture is the CN Tower, the city's most prominent structure, standing 1,815 feet tall.

A speeding monorail as photographed against the night skyline of vibrant Sydney, Australia, in 2002.

The famous skyline of lower Manhattan in the late 1990s, when it still included the twin towers of the World Trade Center.

PITTSBURGH PROMOTES PROGRESS

This postcard image combines a railroad landscape with an urban skyline to showcase the muscle of both Pittsburgh and the mighty Pennsylvania Railroad.

The *American Orient Express* passed several old-fashioned grain elevators, or "prairie skyscrapers," as it sprinted across Saskatchewan.

A foggy morning in Chicago's Loop. The term "The Loop" actually derives from cable cars that looped around downtown blocks in order to reverse direction. The elevated loop, or "L," was not completed until 1897. Since September 11, 2001, zealous guards have made any photography from this location exceedingly difficult.

Portfolio 8

Steel Wheels on Steel Rails

Smoke particles that have been manufactured to exacting specifications form a vital but little appreciated substance called carbon black. The molecules are found in everything from printer toner to high-gloss black paint for automobiles to long-wearing tires. It is hard to imagine that a century ago most of the world's population had never ridden on an air-filled tire. The great bicycle craze of the 1880s and 1890s popularized pneumatic tires, with the French taking the lead in the race for better bicycles and tires. However, when applied to early automobiles, the reworked bicycle tires did not last long. The earliest auto tires squirmed along roadways like giant erasers and wore themselves out in less than two-thousand miles. That changed forever in 1902 when chemists at Michelin discovered that adding carbon black to rubber gave it the long-lasting qualities that we take for granted today.

For most people in 1900, the most modern and efficient wheels were the steel ones that rode on steel rails, the combination that caused streetcars to squeal as they negotiated narrow and twisting city streets. In the realm of urban transportation the world had witnessed many recent technological innovations. During the nineteenth century alone, the rails had evolved from wood to iron to steel, and propulsion of streetcars (or trams) had changed from horse to moving cable to electricity. In the United States the first electrically powered street cars sparked along the streets of Richmond, Virginia, in 1888, only eight years after Thomas Edison invented the incandescent light bulb that for all practical purposes was the opening shot in an electrical revolution. From the beginning the newfangled streetcars were more than mere conveyances: they symbolized modernity itself. Every city, and even some small towns, desired electric streetcars to affirm their status as modern and progressive locations attractive to new businesses and new residents.

Improvements to the technology of long-distance transmission of electricity in the 1890s gave rise to the interurban electric railroad. Instead of streetcar lines serving the needs of city and suburban dwellers, interurban visionaries imagined networks serving states and even regions—and by the early twentieth century that dream became a reality in places as distant as New England and southern California. In time it became possible to ride a variety of electric lines all the way from New York to Chicago, with the exception of a short gap in upstate New York, though the journey required several days and plenty of patience.

One of San Francisco's iconic cable cars, the last representatives of a means of urban transportation popular in many cities across the United States before the introduction of electrically powered cars in the late 1880s. A thick cable ran from a powerhouse along a slot under city streets to provide propulsion. In addition to its cable cars, San Francisco is home to a colorful fleet of historic streetcars.

Henry Huntington made a fortune using his expanding Pacific Electric System to encourage the suburbanization of the greater Los Angeles area.

In physical form the electric interurban lines resembled railroads, though in function they had more in common with automobiles and highways. Across the prairies of Illinois, Indiana, and Ohio they were relatively cheap to build and operate, and the electric cars could easily receive and discharge passengers at any country crossroads. Ultimately, hundreds of companies operated interurban lines in the United States and Canada, yet apart from southern New England, the midwest, and southern California only the sketchiest of networks had emerged by the time the first lines were abandoned. Had the invention of the automobile been delayed by just ten years, the obvious gaps in the network might have been closed and the future of the interurban very different.

In any case, as good as interurban railroads were, automobiles did much the same job, only better; and in terms of long-distance travel, steam railroads remained the speed and comfort champions. With interurban lines typically operating on shoestring budgets, most such carriers withered like pumpkin vines in October when faced with the chilling economic prospects that resulted from automobile competition. By the middle of the 1930s, the Depression Decade, most interurban lines were only memories. Today only one of the original electric carriers survives in the United States. That is the South Shore Line, joining Chicago with South Bend, Indiana, and serving area commuters.

City streetcar lines seemed doomed to suffer the same fate as companies replaced electrically powered cars with gasoline and diesel-powered buses. But in recent years the streetcar in the form of light rail has made a remarkable comeback in cities as distant as St. Louis, San Diego, and Seattle. No city in the United States has greater diversity in urban transportation than San Francisco, which not only maintains its historic cable cars that, according to the popular song, "climb halfway to the stars," but also a variety of classic streetcars, trolley buses, and even a high-speed rail system called the Bay Area Rapid Transit (BART).

Which city in the world has the most extensive network of streetcars or trams? Vienna, Austria, and Melbourne, Australia, are both exceptionally well served by their tram lines. All over Europe, cities have maintained their historic tram lines or added new ones, as Athens did when it hosted the Olympic Games in 2004. Istanbul maintains both a historic streetcar line through one of its main shopping districts and modern tram lines serving other parts of the Turkish metropolis. Along the coast of Belgium an interurban-like tram line connects the area's numerous resort communities. If gasoline prices rise to permanent highs, it is safe to say that streetcar and tram lines will once again loom large in meeting the future transportation needs of world cities.

Steel wheels on steel rails form the essence of metropolitan commuter lines, though Montreal and Paris are two cities that use rubber tires on steel rails to reduce train noise. Most such lines run underground or on elevated tracks to reach the central city. The elevated tracks of Chicago define the famous "Loop" that is the heart of the Illinois metropolis. In addition, Chicago, New York, Philadelphia, Boston, Washington, Los Angeles, Seattle, northern Virginia, and southern Florida all have big-league commuter railroad lines (as distinct from streetcars and light-rail transportation). From Miami International Airport it is possible to ride commuter trains north to Fort Lauderdale and West Palm Beach. The good news for pump-weary motorists is that the

Waiting for a modern streetcar on a rainy night near the stop for Hagia Sophia in December 2007. For nearly five-hundred years it was the main mosque in Constantinople, capital of the Ottoman Empire. Just a few feet to the right of this street-car stop still stands the zero-mile-marker for the Byzantine, or Eastern Roman Empire, also once based in Constantinople, now called Istanbul in Turkish.

number of such systems is increasing: Albuquerque, New Mexico, recently implemented commuter train service to outlying communities north and south of the New Mexico metropolis using diesel locomotives and existing railroad tracks.

As is true also for tram lines, European cities are generally ahead of cities of the United States in supporting dense and extensive networks of commuter trains. No major city on the continent is without them, and they accommodate the twice-daily surge of commuters in many smaller places as well. However, even if the price of gasoline rises to a permanent high, it would be a great mistake to assume that automobiles are doomed. Commuter traffic moving by steel wheels on steel rails will undoubtedly increase, but in the spatially expansive suburbs that define most cities of the United States from Miami to Seattle, commuters will still need to reach the local commuter rail stations in their private automobiles. The Southeastern Pennsylvania Transportation Authority (SEPTA), for example, maintains huge parking lots at its many stations to serve the needs of commuter train riders.

Only an idealist could imagine the demise of the automobile and the complete triumph of steel wheels on steel rails. The automobile of the future will become much more fuel efficient, and using one for long-distance travel across the United States may become an expensive luxury, but because of our suburban sprawl there is no chance that private automobiles will disappear from the urban transportation mix. Nonetheless, I wonder what kind of comeback, if any, the long-distance passenger train will make in America?

SEPTA's busy Convention Center Station in downtown Philadelphia in 2008.

Trams wait outside Vienna's Westbahnhof in the summer of 2007 to take passengers to various parts of Austria's capital city. In all, the city has thirty-one tram lines. Melbourne has the world's largest network of tram lines, but Vienna and Amsterdam rank not far behind the Australian metropolis.

Waiting for a light to change in Budapest, Hungary.

Waiting for a streetcar in Prague, Czech Republic, September 2005. One critic told me to delete this image, but my tightly cropped juxtaposition of human and mechanical forms seems appropriate for a city in which modern buildings, for example, assume the characteristics of human dancers. Two of Prague's most famous entwined buildings have been popularly labeled "Fred Astaire and Ginger Rogers."

Traveling through a leafy park in Krakow, Poland, in the fall of 2005.

The view is from the driver's seat as he eased his train down a narrow-gauge line into Montreux, Switzerland. Positioned between the rails was a line of geared track, part of a rack-and-pinion system that enabled trains to climb or descend unusually steep grades by using cog wheels. The driver governed his speed with a controller that looked much like a steering wheel. The date is May 2007.

Can a trip to Portugal be complete without a thrill ride on an antique street car as it caroms along the narrow and twisting streets of Lisbon?

The empty west: Union Pacific tracks between La Grande and Baker, Oregon, briefly spring to life with a passing freight train in September 1980.

Portfolio 9

The Trouble with Trains

Why did Americans, whose historic passion for train travel was evidenced by their numerous popular songs about it, so unceremoniously dump the luxurious and remarkably safe passenger train to launch a love affair with the winsome but mechanically demanding automobiles of the early and mid-twentieth century? One answer seems obvious. As important as the passenger train and the railroad station once were in the lives of ordinary Americans, they had some serious shortcomings. In truth, not all trains were luxurious. Many of the locals ambling along lightly populated branch-lines or serving main-line towns and villages skipped by the named expresses were track-weary hand-me-downs. There was nothing modern about them, either in their interior appointments or their time consciousness. It is not surprising that some of the first Americans to switch from passenger trains to private automobiles were farm and ranch-dwellers living along railroad branch lines of the Great Plains.

Moreover, for many towns in lightly populated portions of rural America, the train came through but once a day in each direction, and often that was in the wee hours of the night. Especially in the west, main-line schedules were often determined by the railroad's desire to have its long-distance trains arrive in ma-

jor cities at reasonable hours of the day or pass through the most impressive scenery in daylight hours. Sometimes the pressing demand of delivering Uncle Sam's mail on time was the overriding concern in scheduling a train.

A traveling salesman, for example, staying overnight in a small-town hotel might have the desk clerk rap sharply on his door at three in the morning so that he could trundle his heavy samples case to the nearby depot to meet the pre-dawn train, which might be the only one that day going where he was headed next. No wonder traveling salesmen were also among the early riders to abandon the train in favor of the automobile. It was a much more flexible form of transportation in terms of time and space. No longer was he bound by the "tyranny of the timetable" or the spatial arrangements defined by railroad tracks and their trains.

With growing automobile ownership in the years before World War I, families discovered that it was cheaper, and perhaps more fun, to pile into the family car for a trip rather than wait for the train and pay for a ticket for each family member. Gasoline was cheap, and motoring was an adventure. As exasperating as an automobile might be in terms of its mechanical quirks, the "surprise factor" that added zest to a trip was infinitely greater for a car than for a train. Occasionally the surprise was anything but pleasant, as when a car blew a tire or a piston rod, but the machines were relatively simple to fix, and along the road were plenty of seat-of-the-pants mechanics. A delay might even provide a road-weary driver a welcome chance to relax and explore the local community while the car was repaired. Likewise, when a motorist happened on a scenic vista, he/she could easily pull to the side of the road to admire it and perhaps take a picture for the trip scrapbook. No one would dare to ask a conductor to pause his train a few minutes to allow passengers time to admire the scenery. Trains had schedules to keep, and conductors were paragons of industrial discipline.

In the end, it seems that the private automobile addressed the Americans' legendary quest to express their individualism by going where and when they themselves chose to go. Trains, by contrast, followed a corporate model; the important decisions were made in distant offices by experts, with travelers acquiescing to a train's scheduled arrival and departure times and to proper standards of dress, deportment, drinking habits, language, and the like, or risk being summarily ejected at the next station by the almighty conductor, who truly was a "train god." On an Amtrak train I once saw a conductor eject a sloppily dressed young man from the dining car because he insisted on wearing cut-off and patched jeans to the evening meal. By contrast, I suppose that motorists could use McDonald's drive-in window nearly nude if they so desired.

Even with these aforementioned drawbacks, I still enjoy riding trains, though my days of free lunch and travel aboard the *American Orient Express* are a thing of the past. In May 2008 as the price of gasoline edged toward $4 a gallon, I chose to take an Amtrak train from West Palm Beach to Baltimore rather than drive a rental car. Within the confines of my private bedroom aboard the *Silver Meteor* I enjoyed the luxury of an afternoon nap followed by a cooked-to-order dinner that was included in the price of my first-class ticket. From the train windows as we meandered from the Atlantic Coast of Florida to the Gulf Coast and then back again I saw a rural landscape that is scarcely visible from the main freeways with their billboards and look-alike franchised motels and restaurants giving the journey a monotonous sameness.

In all, it took about twenty-six hours to travel from West Palm Beach to Baltimore, but what did I care? I had a quiet room and comfortable bed, handy toilet, hot meals three times a day, a morning newspaper to keep me abreast of latest presidential primary skullduggery (the most boring part of the trip), and my laptop computer. Outside my window the American landscape unfurled—from the swamps of Florida to the piney woods of North Carolina to the broad and history-laden avenues of Washington, D.C. When I finally alighted from my sleeper in Baltimore, the former Pennsylvania station revealed itself to be one of those edifices that bespoke the architectural grandeur of the golden age of railroads. Ironically, through I had ridden many trains along tracks that threaded their way through the Baltimore station's glum and gritty understory, I had never before seen how attractive the building itself was from the street. For me the trouble with trains is that riding them is so relaxing.

"All Aboard!" Amtrak's *Silver Meteor* was about to depart West Palm Beach for points North in May 2008. "All Aboard!"

One of Amtrak's sleek *Acela* trains paused in the Wilmington, Delaware, station in May 2008. The busy "Northeast Corridor" from Washington north to New York and Boston forms the longest stretch of electrified track in the United States.

Patriotic Carter, Wyoming, in October 2002. The lonely settlement is located along the busy main line of the Union Pacific between Chicago and Salt Lake City.

The railroad landscape of Panhandle, near Amarillo, Texas, in November 1990.

On the platform of Copenhagen's Central Station in 2006.

Train companions: these two sisters were members of a family group returning from a day at the beach near Coleraine in Northern Ireland in May 2008.

What was the meaning of railroad space for this traveler aboard an Italian train on its way north from Milan to the resort towns that dot the southern shore of Lake Como?

Old and new: waiting for a train in rural Switzerland.

One of the most terrifying rail journeys anyone ever made was to this town in Poland in the early 1940s. The infamous location is better known to the world today by its German name: Auschwitz.

Achtung! A sign in four languages warns travelers to watch out for trains when crossing the tracks at the Oświecim station in Poland.

Vanishing point: an oncoming Union Pacific train near Bancroft, Idaho, in July 1992.

Portfolio 10
Railroad Art and the Ephemera Collector

Railroads were once avid patrons of the arts, using paintings, photography, and other visual representations to enliven the calendars, promotional brochures, travel guides, and timetables they gave away by the millions—even as railroads themselves became worthy subjects for artists to record on canvas or film. No one today, or even a century ago, could know for certain the total number of individual railroad publications or the size of many print runs. There is no catalog of railroad promotional brochures issued just for the United States in the late nineteenth and early twentieth centuries. However, we can surmise from existing evidence that the number of different brochures easily numbered in the thousands, with cumulative print runs totaling in the millions. Rail companies issued still more brochures extolling the scenic wonders of Canada, Mexico, and a variety of travel destinations in Europe. Railroad posters alone seem to cover every conceivable attraction on six of the world's seven continents.

No worthy subject seemed to escape the interest of America's relentless railroad promoters. In July 1899 the Union Pacific passenger department issued what must rank among the most unusual publications in the annals of railroad literature, and one of the few brochures intended to help transcontinental travelers visualize what lay *beneath* the treeless and windswept landscape of Wyoming, which to travelers accustomed to the wooded and well-watered East must have appeared intolerably barren and bleak.

The title of the Union Pacific booklet was "Some of Wyoming's Vertebrate Fossils." Commenting on the Union Pacific publication, editors of the *Official Guide* noted that "these original inhabitants of Wyoming are attracting great attention from all geologists and paleontologists, and the new discoveries that are constantly being made there are adding materially to scientific knowledge." The Union Pacific "has contributed to this end by publishing the illustrated pamphlet above referred to, and also by issuing invitations (including transportation) to the heads of the scientific departments of the various universities of the country to bring parties to the field for purposes of exploration." Whether the fossil pamphlet was generally available on board its several daily passenger trains across Wyoming is not clear, but interested individuals could easily obtain a free copy by writing to the railroad's home office in Omaha, Nebraska.[11]

11. *Travelers' Official Guide of the Railway and Steam Navigation Lines in the United States, Canada and Mexico* (New York: National Railway Publication Company, July 1899): xxx.

Washington

CHESAPEAKE & OHIO LINES

It would be impossible to identify the most beautiful brochure cover, but this undated one issued by the Chesapeake and Ohio ranks among my favorites.

Railroad brochures devoted to scenery were never value neutral. They were invariably exercises in salesmanship. Railroad publicists, in effect, commodified the American West and numerous other landscapes around the world, much as a dairy might do by promoting its brand of milk, cheese, and ice cream to prospective customers. In the American Southwest, one of the most avid commodifiers was Fred Harvey, who essentially invented the "Southwest Style" or "Santa Fe Style" that remains so popular today in terms of personal dress and interior decoration. Clever wordsmiths, artists, and photographers working for the railroads of the United States not only transformed seemingly worthless lands into the nation's new Gardens of Eden but also made freaks and oddities of nature, like the geysers and mudpots of Yellowstone, into America's answer to the imposing castles, cathedrals, and other tourist attractions of Europe. That is, railroad publicists invented many of the must-see attractions for tourists of the West.

When Congress helped to underwrite the cost of extending the first railroads across the United States in the early 1860s, it did so by providing loans and vast grants of land to the Central Pacific and Union Pacific companies. Congress did likewise in the 1870s for the Northern Pacific, the nation's second transcontinental railroad. If these and other rail companies could coin their landed empires into money, they would have the dollars in hand needed to build and equip their lines, all of which were very expensive. To coin those landed empires into investment capital, railroads were for several decades the most avid promoters of the west. And not just the west.

Many railroads that did not receive federal lands and loans nonetheless had an interest in promoting rapid development of the regions they served. Thus the railroad promotional efforts of the early twentieth century focused on attracting additional people to settle lightly populated portions of the United States, most notably the West but also to the mangrove wilderness that was then southern Florida, and thereby generate additional freight and passenger traffic railroads needed to grow prosperous.

In addition to their myriad publications, America's railroads ran special display cars around the United States to lure farmers and ranchers to settle their new lands. They operated special colonist trains and offered low rates to make relocation easy. Railroads also stepped up efforts to promote tourism as distinct from settlement. The message was essentially: "Come visit our national parks, beaches, and other scenic wonders, and if you like what you see along the way, why not settle out West or in Florida?" Henry Flagler's Florida East Coast Railway and its subsidiaries, for example, did much to promote both tourism and settlement of what became known as the "Sunshine State."

Most early railroad guides confined themselves to describing the passing landscape, noting the rivers, canyons, mesas, and buttes visible from train windows. Some guides enlivened their pages visually by adding a map or two and black and white engravings of local plants and wildlife. Visually, the railroad publications became significantly more vibrant and appealing in the late 1880s and 1890s as major advances in printing technology permitted rail companies to use black and white photographs and an occasional color illustration in their publicity.

Railroad promotion of the passing landscape became even more important as passenger trains traveled faster and the increased speed made it difficult for travelers to study nearby landscapes in detail. In the era of a slow-moving stagecoach, travelers could actually call up to the driver and ask him to pause a moment while they viewed the scenery or marveled at the wildlife—or to shoot it, as was once a common practice on stagecoaches

2192 – A Mammoth Belleflower Apple.

Postcard boosterism featured various tongue-in-cheek depictions of railroads and the oversize fruit or vegetables supposedly grown along their tracks in various agricultural regions of the United States.

A fast freight passes a trackside signal on the former Denver and
Rio Grande Western line at Solitude, Utah, in October 1994.

and trains crossing buffalo country. However, a request to pause for a better look (or a better shot) would have been unthinkable for travelers by train. The engineer located in the cab of a locomotive positioned at the head of a string of passenger cars was physically remote from travelers, and the conductor, who was the real boss of the train, was certainly not willing to deviate from an exacting schedule to accommodate passengers' whims. The physical and mental distance separating travelers and passing landscapes widened as train speeds increased and onboard amenities, like dining cars and air-conditioning, became more generally available.

Railroads used artwork to call public attention to the passing landscape for reasons of its economic appeal to tourists and settlers (and thus plump up a railroad's own bottom line), but they also used illustrations of various types to introduce travelers and prospective passengers to their newest and most innovative equipment and to the modern support structure of tracks and signaling that made travel fast, comfortable, and as safe as possible. In this way, speed and safety gained commercial value along with comfort. Artwork used to promote new trains, improved safety, and the increased creature comforts awaiting travelers for years energized competitive contests between railroads and later with other modes of transportation.[12]

We have no way to know exactly how many people responded to the railroads' ongoing salesmanship. We do know for certain that railroad publicists did have their target audiences. That is,

they engaged in an early form of ethnic and racial profiling. Henry Villard, the German journalist and financier most responsible for completing the Northern Pacific line from Lake Superior to the Pacific Coast, wanted only residents of western and northern Europe to migrate to the northern tier states served by his company. Tons of promotional literature written in German, Danish, Swedish, Norwegian, and like languages reflected that fact. Other railroads did the same. It is not accidental that in parts of the west where railroads did the most to define the demography—the northern tier states from Minnesota to Washington, for instance—that the population still tends to be northern and western European in origin.

The golden age of railroad promotion of tourism and settlement lasted from the 1880s through the 1920s. If anything, the railroads' work of selling the west and Florida went forward even more vigorously from 1900 until the Great Depression than it had during the nineteenth century. Professional railroad publicists organized as the American Railway Development Association in the early twentieth century and held regular meetings for many years to share ideas and assess their salesmanship. In this connection it might be worth noting that more homesteads, as distinct from purchases of railroad land, were filed in the twentieth century than in the nineteenth. The western frontier had supposedly closed in 1890, but it had not in reality.

Though railroad promotional tracts and pamphlets are no longer displayed in station waiting rooms, I religiously stop to search literature racks in hotels for items of interest, and often I bring home heavy quantities in my suitcases. The ephemera is free, like the gasoline company highway maps of years past. State welcome centers, which are more common in the eastern United States than in the west, offer an especially rich lode of

---

12. For a much longer exploration of the meaning of railroad promotional literature, see Carlos A. Schwantes, "The View from the Passenger Car Vestibule: Travelers Interact with the Passing Landscape," *Railroad Heritage* 14 (2005):

Along Your Way

Facts about stations and scenes on the Santa Fe

The cover of a brochure issued by the Atchison, Topeka, and Santa Fe in 1945 highlighted the railway's famous red and yellow "Warbonnet" paint scheme.

NSB

Besøk

JERNBANE MUSEET
HAMAR

ÅPENT HELE ÅRET

NSB - 12/63 - 100 000 - BELL

A page from a brochure issued by the Norwegian state railway in 1963. I religiously search every station for this type of ephemera, and my ongoing quest occasionally has yielded some visual gems.

This photograph shows only a small portion of the collection of books and transportation ephemera amassed by William J. Dixon, who served as president of the Chicago, Rock Island and Pacific Railroad during the years 1970 to 1974.

information on tourist attractions and hence insights into what state and local history is "bankable"—that is, what history has the potential to lure tourist dollars. A century from now the promotional material may prove useful to researchers seeking to know how Americans vacationed in the early twenty-first century or which features of state and local history proved most popular to the casual tourist.[13]

Already collectors of railroad promotional material from the nineteenth century have seen prices of the one-time free-for-the-taking timetables and travel brochures rise above the hundred dollar mark. No so long ago, the same collectable could be had for just a few pennies or a few dollars. One person positioned in the right place and time to build a sizeable personal collection of transportation ephemera was William J. Dixon, president of the Chicago, Rock Island, and Pacific Railroad from 1970 to 1974.

Dixon's remarkable career began on the very bottom rung of the ladder during lean days of the 1930s. Although he had earned a degree in civil engineering from the Pittsburgh school known today as Carnegie Mellon University, he began as a member of a gang of track workers ("gandy dancers" in railroad lingo) on the Pennsylvania main line east of Pittsburgh. During World War II, the United States Army sent him to Iran to facilitate Lend-Lease shipments by rail to Russia and later to Korea to help with the post-war turnover of the nation's railways from Japan. Once again back home in the United States, his career path took him to the Rock Island by way of service on the Baltimore and Ohio. Along the way Dixon pursued an interest in the academic side of

13. Carlos A. Schwantes, "The Case of the Missing Century, or Where Did the American West Go After 1900?" *Pacific Historical Review* 70 (February 2001): 1–20.

railroading with post-baccalaureate study at Yale University and the University of Michigan.

With this background it is not surprising that Dixon developed a passion for the industry's history. Not only does his personal collection contain some unusual railroad promotional brochures, but because Dixon was also interested in architecture he has an outstanding array of pamphlets pertaining to the opening ceremonies of some of the great twentieth century railway stations in the United States. His collection of postcards relating in some way to the railroad landscape includes thousands of images. His collecting passion also encompassed railroad ephemera from Europe and other overseas locations. Thanks to avid collectors like Dixon, a rich visual history as preserved in railroad ephemera will live on for future generations to enjoy.

My own ephemera collection at the St. Louis Mercantile Library is significantly smaller than Dixon's, and I no longer spend my own money to acquire any historic items because the library already owns huge collections of such ephemera. But I do collect for the library the free timetables and rail guides available in European railroad station. The challenge is that such material is highly local in its geographic distribution. Timetables for Luxembourg, for instance, are not likely to be available outside Luxembourg. The situation is likewise for Northern Ireland or for many private railways in Switzerland.

Regional and National timetable compilations comparable to the old *Official Guide* for railways of the United States, Canada, and Mexico are occasionally available for purchase, though the situation varies from country to country. On a 2003 trip to Portugal, I discovered that ticket offices sold for a nominal sum a timetable guide to the country's railways. When I retuned in the summer of 2007, it was no longer available. Portugal's ticket agents told me to check the Internet for train schedules, though small timetables were available for some lines. For travelers wanting the freedom to come and go across Europe on a rail pass, an indispensable companion is a copy of the monthly compilation of European timetables published by Thomas Cook, a successor in many ways to the venerable but now defunct guides first issued by England's George Bradshaw in 1839. The Cook organization also publishes a companion guide covering the rest of the World, including the slim pickings available on railroad lines of the United States and Canada.

Alas, for collectors of transportation ephemera, more and more timetables are available only on the Internet. Amtrak still issues an attractive new systemwide timetable twice a year, but paper timetables for most airlines of the United States have long since disappeared from ticket counters in favor of electronic versions. I was fortunate to have been able to compile a selection of timetables for the airlines of America when they were still available, though it is sobering to realize that most of the air carriers are now history and other legacy carriers of the United States are sure to follow. That somber reality energizes ephemera collectors.

In addition to colorful ephemera that highlights the role railroads once played as patrons of the arts, as important as that visual record is, there is interest among collectors in the way that railroads themselves inspired painters, photographers, novelists, and other creative individuals. Railroad mechanical engineering needs to be recognized as an artistic endeavor, for example: "There is in manufacturing a creative joy that only poets are supposed to know. Some day I'd like to show a poet how it feels to design and build a railroad locomotive." So observed Walter P. Chrysler, a locomotive craftsman before he became an automobile mogul.

But let us return to an even earlier era. One of the most recognizable icons of American fine art is the 1871 oil painting popularly labeled "Whistler's Mother." The artist himself, James McNeill Whistler, called it *Arrangement in Grey and Black: The Artist's Mother*. It hangs today in the Musée d'Orsay in Paris, and therein lies another tale of connections between railroads and the arts, and especially the railroad as art.

The Paris museum is itself a former train station that was skillfully converted from one of France's grand cathedrals of commerce into an equally grand showcase for fine art of the nineteenth century. I especially enjoy impressionist paintings, and works by many of my favorite artists are on display in the Musée d'Orsay. But what seems conspicuously missing is a painting called "Whistler's Father," not that Whistler ever painted one. Yet in his day, George Washington Whistler ranked among the foremost civil engineers in America, and his creativity took flight as a highly innovative series of railroad construction projects, each in its own way a work of art.

A graduate of West Point, the nation's only engineering school until the 1850s, Whistler's father helped lay out the original route of the Baltimore and Ohio Railroad, followed a short time later by the route of the Western Railroad between Boston and Albany, then the longest railroad in the world. In 1842 at the request of Czar Nicholas, he moved his family (including young James) to Russia and for the next seven years labored to overcome the engineering challenges of building a railroad between St. Petersburg and Moscow. "Little Jimmy" was fifteen years old in 1849, the year cholera killed his father.

Railroad structures such as the Thomas Viaduct, a massive

stone structure bridging Maryland's Patapsco River, are examples of George Washington Whistler's engineering art, which might in turn inspire later artists and photographers to capture their grace and symmetry on canvas and film. Painter George Innes included a roundhouse in Scranton, Pennsylvania, in his depiction of the early rail landscape, an 1855 masterpiece he called "The Lackawanna Valley." Examples of the railroad as art could go on and on.[14]

14. A spectacular new book on this subject is Ian Kennedy and Julian Treuherz, *The Railway: Art in the Age of Steam*.

This example of rail ephemera from Australia (ca. 1963) emphasized travel on the country's east-west transcontinental line completed in 1917. The young nation, which dates only from 1901, at long last completed a north-south transcontinental rail line in 2003 that links Adelaide and Darwin.

Abstract art? A Thalys train arrives in Brussels, Belgium, in June 2007.

Who has ever been able to provide an adequate definition of art? In Amsterdam's Rjiksmuseum, one man's art is another's cell-phone conversation.

The juxtaposition of classic station architecture in Strasbourg, France, with the clean lines of modern railway cars makes a statement about the railroad as art. The date is July 2002.

Variation on a theme: a painting of snowcapped mountains and a marmot decorate a
locomotive on Switzerland's "Golden Pass Route" connecting Lucerne and Montreux.

Night in a northern Vermont railway yard in 2002. The light is not the moon but rather a spotlight used to deter theft or vandalism and help railroaders work safely in the dark.

GREAT NORTHERN RAILWAY

SYSTEM TIME TABLE

October 30, 1966 - April 29, 1967

EACH WAY, EVERY DAY BETWEEN
CHICAGO AND THE PACIFIC NORTHWEST

INCOMPARABLE EMPIRE BUILDER
AND MODERN WESTERN STAR

As for the most attractive cover on a railroad timetable, this one issued by the Great Northern in 1966 would rank among my top contenders.

The Baltimore and Ohio Railroad gave away ink blotters, among other ephemera, to advertise its post-World War II streamlined train, the *Cincinnatian*. The new train linked Baltimore and Cincinnati from 1947 to 1950 and Detroit and Cincinnati from 1950 to 1971. Like the train itself, which fell victim to modern technology and failed to survive the advent of Amtrak in 1971, ink blotters, too, vanished from popular use because of competition from ballpoint pens.

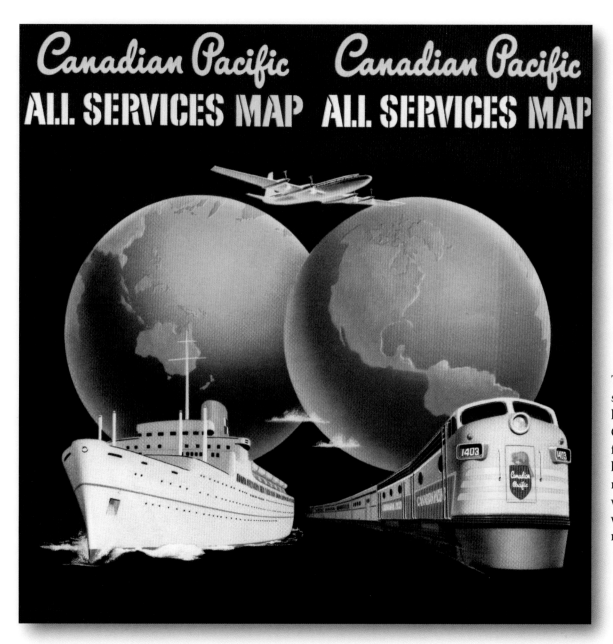

The cover image from a wall map issued by Canadian Pacific in 1957. Unlike railroads in the United States, the Canadian company maintained a far-flung empire of steamship, airline, and hotel subsidiaries in addition to several railroads. One of its railroad holdings was popularly known as the Soo Line, which served Minnesota, Wisconsin, northern Michigan, and North Dakota.

Ready to depart Amtrak's Wilmington, Delaware, station in May 2008 for Philadelphia and points north. Unlike Amtrak stations in Washington, Baltimore, Philadelphia, or New York, tracks through Wilmington are easily accessible and run above ground, thus providing good light to any photographer willing to risk running afoul of local authorities by recording for posterity the ever-fascinating landscape of the railroad.

Conclusion

A moving train next to the stationary one on which Albert Einstein sat in the Bern, Switzerland, station was supposed to have inspired his theory of relativity. Young Sigmund Freud was deathly afraid to ride trains. The father of psychoanalysis, in fact, suffered from acute train phobia. In early 1853 a train crash in Andover, Massachusetts, claimed the life of eleven-year-old Benjamin Franklin Pierce, just one month before his politician father was inaugurated the fourteenth president of the United States. Bennie died as his parents stood helpless, and the tragedy so unhinged the nation's new First Lady that she essentially locked herself in a White House bedroom for the duration of her husband's single term. Jane Pierce came to believe that Bennie died because God punished her husband for accepting the high office of president. It might be argued that the two family tragedies so paralyzed Pierce psychologically that he was incapable of responding in any meaningful way to the unfolding crisis of national unity. Like the train that claimed the life of the Pierces' son, the train of state would lurch wildly along the track until the great Civil War smash up in April 1861.

Often I have wondered about the psychology that may explain a person's fascination with trains. Most rail fans I know do not care to pursue that thought, and yet all of us know that some people can become totally obsessed with trains.[15] One minor French novelist of the nineteenth century describes an engineer who fell deeply in love with his locomotive, only to be destroyed by it. The Freudians could have a speculative field-day with that tale. Some rail fans truly are "foamers," an irreverent term sometimes used to describe an adult who becomes so excited at the sight of an oncoming train that foam begins to form at the corners of his mouth. I say "his" because for some reason the great majority of rail fans are men—though I have encountered a few women who get every bit as excited about trains as men do.

As for me, there may be some deep-seated psychological reason that explains my fascination with trains, though I stop short of calling it an obsession. I simply do not care to spend

15. For a fascinating discussion of this topic see Minsoo Kang, "The Happy Marriage of Steam and Engine Produces Beautiful Daughters and Bloody Monsters: Descriptions of Locomotives as Living Creatures in Modernist Culture, 1875–1935," in Minsoo Kang and Amy Woodson-Boulton, eds., *Visions of the Industrial Age, 1830-1914: Modernity and the Anxiety of Representation in European Culture* (Burlington: Ashgate, 2008): 3–20.

the money to hire a psychoanalyst to find out what that reason might be. I rest content simply to teach a university course called "Railroads in American Life" and to go on photographing and riding trains whenever the opportunity arises. In truth, I am just as happy traveling aboard ships, as I did for the month of September 2007 aboard the *National Geographic Endeavour* as we cruised the Mediterranean from Lisbon to Athens. I think I know why that is.

My father always aspired to be a journalist, but apart from his daily diary and a huge cache of wartime letters to my mother, he never really wrote a sustained essay of which I am aware. However, not long before he died in March 2004 he translated from Portuguese into English the diary entries that describe his one-way voyage north from Santos, Brazil, aboard a Japanese freighter called the *Buenos Aires Maru*. He arrived in San Pedro, California, in the late 1930s as a penniless teenager. Two generations earlier my paternal ancestors traveled from northern Germany to settle in Brazil. In neither case do I know the "whys" of the voyage. However, from these scraps of evidence I am tempted to conclude that imbedded somewhere in our family's biological makeup is a powerful gene inspiring restlessness. Like the legendary Flying Dutchman, a ship captain condemned to sail the seas until judgment day, I am just another "Restless Rider."

The end! In the late 1950s and early 1960s I used my cheap camera to contemplate the empty platform of the Atlantic Coast Line's Wilmington, North Carolina, station. As was typical elsewhere in the United States at the time, sleek observation cars rarely streamlined the blunt end of local trains. Nonetheless, you can be certain that because Wilmington was the railroad's headquarters, luxurious private cars favored by upper management were regularly added to these locals for business trips north to Capitol Hill or Wall Street or south to Florida. In fact, within months after I took these pictures, the railroad relocated its headquarters to Jacksonville, Florida.

Suggestions for Further Reading

Bain, David Haward. *Empire Express: Building the First Trans-continental Railroad.* New York: Viking, 1999.

Chandler, Alfred D., Jr. *Henry Varnum Poor: Business Editor, Analyst, and Reformer.* Cambridge: Harvard University Press, 1956.

Chandler, Alfred D., Jr., ed. *The Railroads: The Nation's First Big Business.* New York: Harcourt, Brace & World, 1965.

Cole, Beverley, and Richard Durack. *Railway Posters, 1923–1947.* York: National Railway Museum, 1992.

Cronon, William. *Nature's Metropolis: Chicago and the Great West.* New York: W. W. Norton & Company, 1991.

Conzen, Michael P. ed. *The Making of the American Landscape.* London: HarperCollins Academic, 1990.

Danly, Susan, and Leo Marx, eds. *The Railroad in American Art: Representations of Technological Change.*Cambridge: The MIT Press, 1988.

Davidson, Janet F., and Michael S. Sweeney. *On the Move: Transportation and the American Story.* Washington: National Geographic, 2003.

Deverell, William. *Railroad Crossing: Californians and the Railroad, 1850–1910.* Berkeley: University of California Press, 1994.

Douglas, George H. *All Aboard! The Railroad in American Life.* New York: Marlowe & Company, 1995.

Ellis, C. Hamilton. *The Royal Trains.* London: Routledge and Kegan Paul Ltd., 1975.

Freeman, Michael. *Railways and the Victorian Imagination.* New Haven and London: Yale University Press, 1999.

Gordon, Sarah. *Passage to Union: How Railroads Transformed American Life, 1829–1929.* Chicago: Ivan R. Dee, 1997.

Grant, H. Roger. *The North Western: A History of the Chicago & North Western Railway System.* DeKalb: Northern Illinois University Press, 1996.

Grant, H. Roger. *"Follow the Flag:" A History of the Wabash Railroad Company.* Dekalb: Northern Illinois University, 2004.

———, Don L. Hofsommer, and Osmund Overby. *St. Louis Union Station: A Place for People, A Place for Trains.* St. Louis: St. Louis Mercantile Library, 1994.

Jackson, John Brinckerhoff. *American Space: The Centennial Years: 1865–1876.* New York: Norton, 1972.

Hofsommer, Don L. *Minneapolis and the Age of Railways.* Minneapolis: University of Minnesota Press, 2005.

———. *The Southern Pacific, 1901–1985.* College Station: Texas

A&M University Press, 1986.

———. *The Tootin' Louie: A History of the Minneapolis & St. Louis Railway*. Minneapolis: University of Minnesota Press, 2004.

Hudson, John C. *Chicago: A Geography of the City and Its Region*. Chicago: University of Chicago Press, 2006.

———. "Railroads and Urbanization in the Northwestern States." In William L. Lang, ed., *Centennial West: Essays on the Northern Tier States*, 169–93. Seattle: University of Washington Press, 1991.

Jackson, John Brinckerhoff. *Discovering the Vernacular Landscape*. New Haven: Yale University Press, 1984.

Jonnes, Jill. *Conquering Gotham. A Gilded Age Epic: The Construction of Penn Station and Its Tunnels*. New York: Viking, 2007.

Kennedy, Ian, and Julian Treuherz. *The Railway: Art in the Age of Steam*. New Haven: Yale University Press, 2008.

Klein, Maury. *Unfinished Business: The Railroad in American Life*. Hanover: University Press of New England, 1994.

Lass, William E. *A History of Steamboating on the Upper Missouri*. Lincoln: University of Nebraska Press, 1962.

Lubetkin, M. John. *Jay Cooke's Gamble: The Northern Pacific Railroad, the Sioux, and the Panic of 1873*. Norman: University of Oklahoma Press, 2006.

Lyden, Anne M. *Railroad Vision: Photography, Travel, and Perception*. Los Angeles: J. Paul Getty Museum, 2003.

Martin, Albro. *James J. Hill and the Opening of the Northwest*. New York: Oxford University Press, 1976.

———. *Railroads Triumphant: The Growth, Rejection & Rebirth of a Vital American Force*. New York: Oxford University Press, 1992.

Meinig, D. W., ed. *The Interpretation of Ordinary Landscapes*. New York: Oxford University Press, 1979.

Orsi, Richard J. *Sunset Limited The Southern Pacific Railroad and the Development of the American West, 1850-1930*. Berkeley: University of California Press, 2005.

Overton, Richard C. *Burlington West: A Colonization History of the Burlington Railroad*. Cambridge, MA: Harvard University Press, 1941.

Pomeroy, Earl. *In Search of the Golden West: The Tourist in Western America*. New York: Alfred A. Knopf, 1957.

Renehan, Edward J., Jr. *Commodore: The Life of Cornelius Vanderbilt*. New York: Basic Books, 2007.

Richter, Amy G. *Home on the Rails: Women, the Railroad, and the Rise of Public Domesticity*. Chapel Hill: University of North Carolina Press, 2006.

Riegel, Robert Edgar. *The Story of Western Railroads: From 1852 through the Reign of the Giants*. New York: Macmillan, 1926.

Runte, Alfred. *Allies of the Earth: Railroads and the Soul of Preservation*. Kirksville: Truman State University, 2006.

———. *Trains of Discovery: Western Railroads and the National Parks*. Rev. ed. Niwot, Colo.: Roberts Rinehart, 1990.

Schivelbusch, Wolfang. *The Railway Journey: Trains and Travel in the 19th Century*. New York: Urizen Books: 1979.

Schwantes, Carlos Arnaldo. "*Everything I Needed to Know About Life I Learned from the Pennsy*." Saint Louis: John W. Barriger III National Railroad Library, 2001.

———. *Going Places: Transportation Redefines the Twentieth-Century West*. Bloomington and Indianapolis: Indiana University Press, 2003.

———. *Long Day's Journey: The Steamboat & Stagecoach Era in the Northern West*. Seattle and London: University of Washington Press, 1999.

———. *Railroad Signatures Across the Pacific Northwest.* Seattle and London: University of Washington Press, 1993.

———, and James P. Ronda, *The West the Railroads Made.* Seattle: University of Washington Press, 2008.

Scott, Roy V. *Railroad Development Programs in the Twentieth Century.* Ames: Iowa State University Press, 1985.

Simmons, Jack, and Gordon Biddle, eds. *The Oxford Companion to British Railway History.* Oxford: Oxford University Press, 1999.

Stilgoe, John R. *Common Landscape of America, 1580–1845.* New Haven: Yale University Press, 1982.

———. *Metropolitan Corridor: Railroads and the American Scene.* New Haven and London: Yale University Press, 1983.

———. *Train Time: Railroads and the Imminent Reshaping of the United States Landscape.* University of Virginia Press, 2007.

Stover, John F. *American Railroads.* 2d ed. University of Chicago Press, 1997.

Taylor, George Rogers, and Irene E. Neu. *The American Railroad Network 1861-1890.* University of Illinois Press, 2003.

Tuan, Yi-Fu. *Topophilia: A Study of Environmental Perception, Attitudes, and Values.* Englewood Cliffs, NJ: Prentice-Hall, 1974.

Vance, James E., Jr. *The North American Railroad: Its Origin, Evolution, and Geography.* Baltimore: Johns Hopkins University Press, 1995.

Ward, James A. *Railroads and the Character of America, 1820-1887.* Knoxville: University of Tennessee Press, 1986.

Acknowledgments

Colleagues who deserve to be thanked for their help include John Neal Hoover, Director of the St. Louis Mercantile Library at the University of Missouri-St. Louis, who published some of my earliest personal reflections on trains and travel in a booklet with the tongue-in-cheek title, *Everything I Needed to Know About Life I Learned from the Pennsy.* Gregory P. Ames, curator at the John W. Barriger III National Railroad Library at the Mercantile Library, has long encouraged me to do something public with my rapidly expanding collection of transportation photographs. Dr. Ray Mundy, director of the Center for Transportation Studies, has also long encouraged my work and generously supported my travel habit. I hope this book is only the first fruit that results from my somewhat unorthodox practice of learning all I can in a research library and then traveling far and wide to gather added materials for my classes "American Railroads in Global Perspective" and "Saint Louis and the West." Finally, special thanks go to Ron Goldfeder, a student from the former class who has been of immense help over the years.

I took and selected all photographs used in *Just One Restless Rider.* Together with the various ephemera illustrations, they are contained in the "Carlos A. Schwantes Collection of Transportation and Travel Ephemera," a growing assortment of historical materials available to users at the St. Louis Mercantile Library. That library, I firmly believe, preserves and houses the largest collection of transportation-related documents and images in the United States, if not the world.

Index